ARGONAUT

Number Four:
West Texas A&M University Series
Jerry Craven, General Editor

Simon Lake, ca. 1938

Argonaut

The

Submarine Legacy of Simon Lake

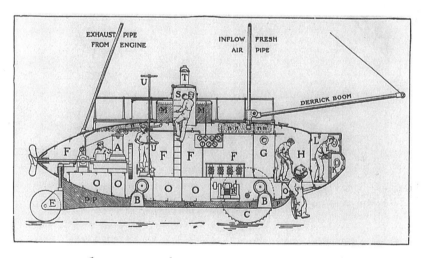

John J. Poluhowich

Texas A&M University Press
College Station

For Bobbie,
who has never faltered in her support,
and Gene,
teacher, mentor, friend.

Copyright © 1999 by John J. Poluhowich
Manufactured in the United States of America
All rights reserved
First edition

The paper used in this book meets the minimum requirements of the American National
Standard for Permanence of Paper for Printed Library Materials, Z39.48-1984.
Binding materials have been chosen for durability.
∞

Library of Congress Cataloging-in-Publication Data

Poluhowich, J. (John)
    Argonaut : the submarine legacy of Simon Lake / John J. Poluhowich.
      p. cm.—(West Texas A&M University series ; no. 4)
    Includes bibliographical references and index.
    ISBN 0-89096-894-2
    1. Lake, Simon, 1866–1945.   2. Naval architects—United States—Biography.   3. Sub-
marines (Ships)—History.   I. Title.
II. Series.
VM14.L25P65   1999
623.8′1′092—dc21
  [B]   99-14479
                                                            CIP

Contents

Illustrations

Acknowledgments

The following narrative is the culmination of a lifelong interest and fascination with the underwater environment. The number of people who have contributed to and sustained this fascination is extensive. To those I miss in these acknowledgments, my apologies.

Heading the list is my wife, Roberta. To say thank you to her for the numerous contributions to this and my other works in a manner befitting her input would require that I employ every complementary adjective in the dictionary. Her ability to sustain so much of my nonsense is heroic if not monumental. None of the accomplishments that go to my credit would have been possible without her constant love, devotion, and caring.

Another individual who played a significant role in this, and in many of my other undertakings, is Dr. Michael E. (Gene) Somers, former chairman of the Biology Department at the University of Bridgeport. It was this gentle man and scholar who suggested that I turn my boyhood interests into the pages that follow. Gene is that exceptional teacher who markedly affects the lives of all around him, especially his students. He is one of the few people to whom I owe more than a simple debt of gratitude.

Senior Chief Petty Officer Grace Glenn ("G_2") is of particular significance to the writing of this book. It was through her efforts that I was invited to the launching of the USS *Rickover* on August 27, 1983, and to travel aboard the attack submarine USS *Philadelphia*. What also added to this chronicle were the historical and political characterizations that she and Captain Marshall Phillips of the U.S. Coast Guard provided during our many discussions.

Former members of the staff of the Submarine Force Library and Museum in Groton, Connecticut, who provided assistance as well as a great deal of information used in this book include Senior Chief Petty Officer Robert Zollars, Staff Assistant Dave Bishop, and Master Chief Gary Morrison. Captain Donal Knepper, former commanding officer of the U.S.

Submarine Base at New London, Connecticut, was also helpful in my endeavors. I am grateful for the assistance of Mr. John Vajda, Ms. Katherine Bowman, and Dr. D.C. Allard of the Naval Historical Center, Operational Archives Branch, Washington Navy Yard, Washington, D.C., and Richard von Doenhoff of the Reference Branch. The staff members of the National Archives in Washington, D.C., are also recognized for their invaluable assistance in amassing the large number of documents required to complete this book.

Special thanks and recognition are due Thomas Alva Edison Lake, son of Simon Lake, who gave freely of his time and provided me with his personal insights into his father's accomplishments. The many hours I spent with him were both informative and enjoyable. Tom died on December 7, 1979. Another Lake family member, Jeffrey Lake, curator of the Simon Lake Collection in Grant, Florida, also provided considerable information and documentation about the activities of Simon Lake.

The University of Bridgeport and the Mellon Foundation provided gracious support during the compilation of the materials needed to write this book.

Numerous individuals at West Texas A&M University provided valuable assistance during this undertaking. Most notably are Dr. Douglas Bingham, Dr. Horace Bailey, Laura Marshall, Madeleine Tainton, and Janie Silva. The staff of the reference section of the Cornette Library is thanked for fulfilling the numerous requests I filed.

I also thank my parents, John and Alice, for their support and encouragement (especially during my early diving years), as well as my brother, Bill, who always seemed to be present with his camera.

Two individuals in particular require singular acknowledgment for their efforts that ensured that this work was completed. Dr. Jerry Craven, professor of English at West Texas A&M University, is responsible for kick-starting my desire to have this story see daylight and served as my editor-in-residence. I am grateful to Noel R. Parsons, editor-in-chief of the Texas A&M University Press, for his kind assistance and, especially, his patience.

ARGONAUT

Introduction

Ar-go-naut (ar′-gə-not′). n. [L. Argonauta;
Gr. Argonautes] 1. in Greek legend, any of the men
who sailed with Jason to search for the Golden Fleece.
2. a person who took part in the California gold rush
of 1848–49. 3. in zoology, the **paper nautilus,** an eight-
armed mollusk related to the octopus.

—Webster's New World Dictionary
of the American Language

A paper nautilus, that's all it was at the start. As the young Simon Lake studied the crude pencil sketch before him, his imagination began to animate his drawing. The submarine crawled over the sea bottom, its metal wheels carving deep ruts into the mud. Searchlights sliced through the murky water, illuminating its path. The craft slowed to a halt as the rotting timbers of a hulk rose before it. A diver emerged from the pressurized chamber in the bow of the submarine and moved, as if in slow motion, to the wreck site. Brushing aside the sediments that had accumulated over the centuries, the diver exposed a large chest and then snapped its rusty lock with a pry bar. The diver's eyes widened at the sight of the glittering treasure within.

The fantasy completed, Lake folded his drawing and placed it into his copy of Jules Verne's *Twenty Thousand Leagues Under the Sea.* He was just a boy when he read Verne's classic adventure story and sketched his idea for a submarine. But the red-headed kid from Pleasantville, New Jersey,

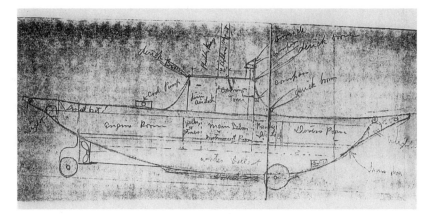

fig. 1. One of Lake's earliest known pencil sketches of a submarine. Courtesy
Thomas A. E. Lake

would live that dream and contribute greatly to the submarine's development as both an instrument of war and a tool of peace.[1]

Attempting to unravel the life and times of an inventor is akin to un-
screwing the hinges of Pandora's Box while trying to prevent the lid from
springing open. This is particularly true for American inventors of the
early nineteenth and twentieth centuries, who were required to deal with
the expanding Washington bureaucracy and its numerous Tammany-like
politicians and industrialists. Endowed with generous amounts of purpose, foresight, and idiosyncrasy, inventors were rarely appreciated or fully
understood by the unimaginative bureaucrats who were in positions to
pass judgment upon their work. "America invents and Europe capitalizes"
was the all too familiar quip of inventors at the turn of the century, reflecting the shortcomings of the U.S. government and industry at the time.
The plight of men like Robert Fulton and the Wright brothers attests to
the validity of the statement. They, like many of the most creative minds
of the time, were forced to emigrate to Europe to witness the fruition of
their dreams. It was a difficult period for such expatriate visionaries, particularly in light of the the nationalistic feelings that were growing in the
United States. The Civil War had laid open deep wounds in the country,
and although the period of healing was painfully slow, Reconstruction and
the concomitant need for new technologies brought forth a profusion of
inventive skills honed on the lessons of the Industrial Revolution and the
desire to expand America's technological base. Patriotism and the pride of

accomplishment were again becoming a way of life throughout the country. The thought of having to implement their inventive labors in Europe was a major source of consternation for many U.S. inventors.[2]

Enter onto this scene Simon Lake. He was the classic American inventor, an enigma whose contributions to history have been variously described by different writers. For example, the British naval historian Richard Compton-Hall says of Lake: "He had a demoniacal sense of the absurd and a recognition of good theatre which would have made him memorable even if he never invented anything worthwhile."[3] Contrast this description with that of Herbert Corey, who stated: "Perhaps no man in the past century has had as much to do with the shape of history as Simon Lake. That statement is intended as a query rather than as a statement. It may be debatable, but it is also defendable."[4]

Part of the confusion regarding the contributions of Simon Lake and the unique manner in which they were often accomplished resides in the lack of a thorough study of his life. His ghostwritten autobiography,[5] according to his son Thomas A. E. Lake,[6] was written with little input by Lake and was a book he was extremely unhappy with when it appeared in 1938. Lake's own book, *The Submarine in War and Peace,* covers only his early involvement with submarine construction and his visions for its future.[7] Numerous other sources, however, leave little doubt that he contributed significantly to the development of the modern submarine.[8]

Lake would use his early submarines to amass a fortune by salvaging sunken cargoes from Long Island Sound and would become one of Connecticut's leading multimillionaires. His work was to provide impetus for the development and military use of the submarine in Europe, particularly in Russia and Germany during the First and Second World Wars. While constructing submarines in Russia, he would, on several occasions, dine and attend the opera with Czar Nicholas II. His work afforded him the opportunity to deal with such notables as President Theodore Roosevelt, then-Secretary of the Navy Franklin D. Roosevelt, the deep-sea explorer William Beebe, and Clara Barton, founder of the Red Cross. While in Europe he would share offices with the Wright brothers. Only after considerable political embattlement was he permitted to build military submarines for his own country.

His descent from prominence would be the combined result of the antisubmarine mania following World War I and Lake's desire to return to his earlier efforts to reap the resources of the sea. Lake ultimately dissipated his fortune in a number of unsuccessful ventures, one of which in-

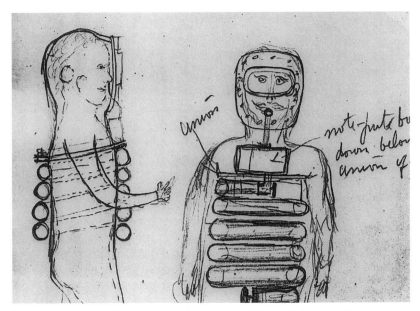

fig. 2. One of Lake's early sketches, dated 1893 and depicting a design for a self-contained breathing apparatus to free hard-hat divers of their cumbersome hoses. Courtesy Thomas A. E. Lake

volved his attempt to salvage the multimillion-dollar payroll that reportedly had sunk with the British man-of-war HMS *Hussar* at Hell Gate, New York, during the American Revolution. He would be involved in one of the first attempts to reach the North Pole by submarine. During World War II he tried to interest President Franklin D. Roosevelt in the construction of large transport submarines as a more effective and safer mode of troop and equipment transport than ship convoys. After the closure of his submarine plant, the Lake Torpedo Boat Company, he would turn his creative powers to the construction of inexpensive quality homes, as one of the first to consider the use of prefabricated housing.

R. S. Barker described Simon Lake as "a stout-shouldered, powerfully built man, in the prime of life, a man of cool common sense, a practical man who is also an inventor. And he talks frankly and convincingly and yet modestly of his accomplishments."[9] His accomplishments were many, as were his battles with Washington and naval bureaucrats. In retrospect, history has lost sight of his significance. The recognition afforded him by the U.S. Government occurred only after his death, in 1945. Nineteen years later, in 1964, a Polaris submarine tender was christened in his name. The cost of this vessel alone ($73 million) exceeded that of all the submarines Lake ever built. For many years after his death, the *Explorer,* his personal vest-pocket research submarine and the only extant example of his work, stood in a weed-infested field behind a Little League field in Milford, Connecticut. Fortunately, this submarine was retrieved and refurbished and, for a number of years, resided at the Submarine Force Library and Museum at the U.S. Naval Submarine Base in Groton, Connecticut. Subsequently, the *Explorer* was placed on display at the New London memorial to the USS *Nautilus,* the world's first atomic submarine. The numerous displays at this memorial chronicling the history of the submarine sparsely mentioned Lake's role in its development. Few of the naval personnel training for submarine duty at Groton understood the significance of these memorabilia, and many failed to even recognize the name Simon Lake.

In 1998, the *Explorer* was returned to her home in Milford, Connecticut, and placed on exhibit at the Milford Public Library. Besides the rotting pilings that still exist in Bridgeport Harbor, Connecticut, and from which numerous submarines were launched in the early 1900s, the only other remnant of Lake's work lies rusting a few miles away in Milford Harbor. The hulk is all that remains of the unique salvage tube that Lake used for treasure hunting. It usually raises the curiosity of weekend boaters as they cruise past it, knowing nothing of its fascinating history.

Whether the activities of Simon Lake represent "a demoniacal sense of the absurd and a recognition of good theatre" or contributions whose significance is "debatable but . . . also defendable" will be left to the reader.

CHAPTER 1

The Pitch Pine Submarine

What one man can imagine, another can create.
—*Jules Verne in a letter to his father.*

The winter wind wrinkled the surface of the Shrewsbury River in the Atlantic Highlands of New Jersey. It was December of 1894. Simon Lake and a cousin, Bart Champion, released their flatiron-shaped wooden craft into the water, cautiously watching as it settled to its waterline. It was an unceremonious launching at best. There was no brass band or crowd of spectators, no champagne bottle broken over the bow for fear of rupturing the thin pine boards that composed her hull.

This primitive submarine was a prototype constructed on a shoestring budget to substantiate the claims of its inventor and to demonstrate its feasibility to future investors. A year earlier, at the age of twenty-seven, Lake had entered a U.S. government competition for military submarine designs. His design had been rejected in favor of those submitted by an Irish inventor named John Holland. Disappointed but undeterred, Lake set about building a prototype with which to test his theories of underwater navigation and exploration. His initial fascination with submarines, which stemmed from his reading of Jules Verne's *Twenty Thousand Leagues Under the Sea,* had instilled in him the desire to salvage sunken cargoes and reap the resources of the sea. The thought of constructing a submarine for warring purposes was secondary to his mission. As Lake saw it, the government's call for military designs provided an opportunity for an inventor to establish himself as a submarine constructor. Once the military aspects of the work were accomplished, he could return to his initial

fig. 3. The first newspaper photograph of the *Argonaut Jr.* as she appeared in 1894. The photograph was retouched to enhance details. Courtesy Thomas A. E. Lake

interests of salvage and exploration. Rejected and unable to procure government support, Lake would seek private funding. The wooden prototype would demonstrate the validity of his design.

Christened the *Argonaut Junior,* she was only 14 feet long, 4 1/2 feet wide, and 5 feet high, with a displacement of seven tons. According to Lake, he had called this experimental craft the *Junior* because she was "born before its mother," the *Argonaut,* which was to have been a much larger steel submersible.[1] Erroneously, he thought that the animal called the paper nautilus (scientifically, *Argonauta*) was the dangerous Portuguese man-of-war. He therefore considered *Argonaut* to be a fitting name for his submarine because it could, with modifications, be converted from a salvage craft into an effective mine-laying coastal defense submarine. Ironically, the docile and peaceful paper nautilus more closely resembles in its manner Lake's early intent for submarines, the nonmilitary exploration of the ocean bottom and harvesting of its riches. In his autobiography he explained, "I had worked out the scheme for the Lake submarine and had decided to name it the *Argonaut,* if and when I was able to build one. At this time I had no thought of building a submarine for naval use. I

fig. 4. Simon Lake's grandfather posing on the discarded hull of the *Argonaut Jr.* some years after she had been abandoned. Courtesy Thomas A. E. Lake

was possessed of my original conviction that a submarine built for purely commercial use would be profitable."[2] He was further intrigued that his submarine bore the designation of a nautilus, which equated with the fictitious craft captained by Jules Verne's Nemo. However, unlike Nemo, whose submarine was designed for both exploration and defense, Lake would encounter serious difficulties in attempting to separate these roles. His efforts to prove that his designs were versatile enough to be incorporated into either salvage submarines or military craft would bring a Janus-like result: his salvaging submarines would be largely successful; his involvement with the military would prove difficult, especially in attempting to gain government acceptance of the submarines he would submit. This conflict of purpose would plague his career as a constructor of submarines.

Financial constraints prevented the *Junior* from being constructed of steel. Instead, she was built entirely of thin yellow pine timber, double thick with canvas sandwiched between the layers, and painted with coal tar to seal the seams. Many of Lake's contemporaries would refer to her as the "pitch pine" submarine. For anyone viewing this contraption, it would have been difficult to envision it as an undersea craft. The hull was mounted on wheels, a characteristic trademark of Lake's early submarines.

These wheels and the unique diving chamber for underwater exit onto the sea bottom were two features of Lake submarines that caused a good deal of anguish in individuals unfamiliar with diving principles. Lake was often asked what would happen if the submarine wheeled off an underwater cliff. His reply of "nothing," was disconcerting to most who did not realize that the small negative buoyancy of the craft would simply let it drift over the edge, where it would slowly sink a short distance to its neutral buoyancy point and then continue on its way suspended in the water at a slightly lower level. The idea of opening a hatch while the craft was submerged was completely foreign to the thinking of most people of the day. They could not understand the fact that no water would enter if the air pressure within the submersible were equal to that of the surrounding seawater. What made for a very interesting situation was that many of the people unable to comprehend these principles were U.S. Navy officials. But this was the time of the submarine's infancy, and few were familiar with underwater phenomena.[3]

Submarines and surface vessels float on the water because they have positive buoyancy. For a submarine to dive, water is flooded into the ballast tanks, reducing its buoyancy to a neutral condition, whence it is driven underwater by the propulsion system and diving planes. To raise the craft to the surface, compressed air is released into the ballast tanks, forcing the water out. It is a simple principle on paper but can become complicated in practice, and a good deal of engineering skill is required to design a successful and safe submarine. Lake incorporated a ballasting system in the *Junior* that permitted the craft to descend on an even keel. He thought this method of diving was superior to that used by his contemporaries who relied upon the forward motion of the vessel to drive it underwater in a porpoise-like fashion. Lake considered this "porpoising" maneuver dangerous, believing that it could result in the craft's striking and possibly becoming embedded in the bottom mud. Although many naval officials would disagree with him, it should be recalled that, at this point in time, submarines were essentially running blind. The periscope, sonar, and the sophisticated electronic sounding devices of modern submarines had yet to be invented. Even-keel diving, according to Lake, would greatly enhance the safety of submarines. To further increase the control of horizontal stability of a submarine during its dive, Lake proposed the use of hydroplanes, wing-like devices that resembled the elevators on the tails of modern aircraft. He did not employ these on the *Junior* because of her simplicity and small size, but later he would use them on his larger submarines. His constant concern for safety caused him to incorporate a drop keel into the *Junior*. Should the craft encounter difficulty in surfacing, the detachable lead keel could be released, increasing the submarine's buoyancy and permitting her to rise safely to the surface.[4]

Diving and surfacing in a submarine are one thing. The craft must also be propelled laterally through the water, and it was this propulsion problem that had hindered the development of the submarine as an effective underwater vehicle. In the 1890s, diesel engines had not yet been invented, and electric motors were very primitive and barely powerful enough to drive a submarine. The internal combustion engine had been developed, but its explosive gasoline fuel, coupled with its carbon monoxide exhaust, made it a questionable source of power. Further, its high demand for oxygen placed heavy requirements upon a submarine's air supply when submerged. The 1890s were the heyday of the steam engine, and steam was standard. Although steam engines were used on a number of submarines for propulsion, the intense temperatures developed within the craft usually made them uninhabitable for the crew. To drive the *Argonaut Junior*, Lake had to use the other power source of the day—muscle. He employed an internal crank to turn the wheels of his craft once it reached the bottom.[5] The *Junior* was designed to go straight to the bottom on an even keel and then crawl along the substratum on her wheels.

To keep construction costs down, Lake purchased soda fountain tanks from a bankrupt drug store and used them to contain the compressed air needed for ballast control in the *Junior*. These tanks were capable of holding 100 psi, which provided enough air to permit the prototype to function at a maximum depth of twenty feet. Lake used a secondhand plumber's hand pump to fill these tanks with air. He needed diving gear to demonstrate the usefulness of his diving chamber, through which a diver could exit the submarine to explore the sea bottom. Lacking funds to purchase such equipment, Lake hammered out a bucketlike diving helmet equipped with a deadlight from a yacht's window to serve as a faceplate and fashioned a crude diving suit from painted canvas. He would tie window sash weights to his legs to keep himself upright on the bottom. The result of Lake's efforts was a craft that appeared to be the ramshackle apparatus of a crazy inventor. However, the *Junior*, as crude as she might have appeared, would serve to demonstrate Lake's understanding of diving principles and his ability to implement them.[6]

The first dive with the *Junior* proved to be somewhat nerve-racking for Bart Champion but apparently not for Lake. The undaunted inventor would state many years later that he never knew fear in one of his submarines, especially when he had control of her. The two argonauts paddled the *Junior* to an area on the river called Blackfish Hole and prepared to dive. The hatch was closed and the ballast tanks flooded. As the craft began to sink, a stream of water hit Champion in the back of the head. A bolt hole in the hull had not been sealed, and water was shooting through it into the interior. For reasons he could not explain, Champion leapt toward the light from a six inch porthole that had been built into the bow of the sub. Upon reaching it, he quickly realized that there was no way he could escape through this small opening. Before Champion's panic was fully realized, Lake nonchalantly plugged the bolt hole with a piece of wood. The problem solved, the *Junior* continued her descent to the bottom, and Champion's fear subsided for the moment.[7]

The wooden wheels of the craft sank into the soft muddy bottom before gaining a solid foothold in the underlying packed mud. Reduced light at a depth of twenty feet created an eerie sensation because the *Junior* did not contain a lighting system. Once their eyes grew accustomed to the darkened environment, the two neophyte submariners started turning the crank. The prototype began to crawl along the river bottom on its first underwater odyssey. It was an exhilarating experience, even for Bart Champion.

After a short period of testing, Lake decided it was time to open the diver's hatch that would permit him to view and work directly on the bottom. He made some rapid calculations and raised the pressure inside the sub. Without hesitation, he reached for the latch. In the dimmed environment, Champion's face paled, but his growing confidence in his cousin's engineering abilities prevented him from offering any objection. There was a hiss as trapped air was expelled from under the hatch. Champion glanced quickly at the main hatch, through which he had entered the submarine. Lake let out a burst of quiet laughter, gloating with satisfaction as he laid back the diver's hatch. Below him was the bottom mud, rich in clams and other estuarine forms. A small fish curiously swam by.[8]

During the next few weeks, Lake and Champion made numerous dives, testing and refining their small craft. Finally, on January 6, 1895, a public demonstration of the *Argonaut Junior* was held. Advance news articles attracted many of Lake's neighbors in the Atlantic Highlands as well as individuals from more distant locations. The press attended in significant numbers (an important, planned part of Lake's intent to gain recognition as an inventor and builder of submarines). Also in the crowd were several people he hoped would invest in his newly formed Lake Submarine

Company, which would permit him to construct the *Junior*'s mother, the larger *Argonaut*.[9]

As the crowd gathered, Lake and Champion boarded the *Junior* and let her drift from the dock into the center of the river. The hatch was closed and the submarine sank below the surface. The crowd became increasingly quiet as the minutes passed. Within a short time, the *Junior* broke the surface, and Lake cheerfully waved to the crowd. The day would witness several more dives with the small prototype, demonstrating that it could prowl the bottom and surface long distances from the shore. When they returned to the dock, the submariners held up various objects that they had retrieved from the bottom. Hearing words of skepticism suggesting that these objects had been secreted on board the *Junior* prior to her submersion, Somers Champion, one of Lake's uncles, proposed a test. He had the mayor and other dignitaries present sign their names on a shingle, attached it to a sash weight, and threw it into the river. Lake understood the challenge and reentered his submarine. The *Junior* dove to the bottom in sixteen feet of water. Within five minutes after diving, Lake was again at the surface, this time waving the shingle triumphantly to the crowd. He had made believers of the doubting Thomases on the shore and went home that day believing that the *Junior* could do anything he claimed for it.[10] Simon Lake had partially fulfilled his boyhood dream —he had indeed become an Argonaut, and, like Jason, he was ready to go in quest of gold.

News coverage of Lake's accomplishment hovered between skepticism and amusement. The media seemed to be asking, "What of it?" The *New York Herald* reported:

> This Boat Crawls along the Bottom. At Least That's What It Was to Do, but It Escapes and Astonishes Folks in Oceanic, N.J.
>
> DRIFTS UP THE SHREWSBURY
>
> IT WILL CRAWL FIVE MILES WITHOUT COMING UP TO BREATHE WHEN INVENTOR LAKE COMPLETES IT. FUN FOR THE MERMEN
>
> ---
>
> RED BANK, N.J., Jan 8, 1895.—Strange things come in with the tide in the ungodly hours of the night, and in the stillness of the night strange things follow them, but the strange thing which came up the North Shrewsbury a day or two ago, and which lies high and dry on Barley Point, is a "new one" on the good folk of Oceanic. Now that they have fairly discovered it, they are

sorry it didn't wobble ashore in the summer, when Normandie-
by-the-Sea below the point is crowded with curious persons
from the city. Any enterprising Oceanic man might have fenced
in the queer thing and charged every one a quarter to see it.[11]

Another article, appearing in a Philadelphia newspaper, would bother
Lake for years after the public demonstration of the *Junior*. It sarcastically
indicated that Lake would patrol the bottom of the sea, plucking up trea-
sures that had accumulated over the centuries, making "Croesus, Barney,
Barrato, the Rothschilds and all the other rich men whose names the reporter could remember . . . paupers by comparison to Simon Lake."[12]
Some years later upon encountering this reporter again, Lake began to
admonish him for his apparent ridicule only to learn that the reporter
had been sincere in his earlier writing and was now boasting about his
predictions of Lake's accomplishments.

Until 1893, Lake's childhood plans for the *Argonaut* had remained a
fantasy of numerous daydreams. But the times were changing, as were the
U.S. Navy's convictions regarding submarines. Five years before Lake had
constructed the *Argonaut Junior,* the navy had made the first of three announcements for submarine competitions.[13] Grover Cleveland was president. His secretary of the navy, William. C. Whitney, had been persuaded
by Montgomery Sicard, chief of the Bureau of Ordnance, and Lieutenant
Commander William. W. Kimball, a staunch proponent of submarine
construction by the U.S. Navy, of the need to investigate the military use
of submarines because of progress then being made in Europe. Unknown
to Lake and most of the other competitors who would make one or more
submissions during these open competitions, Lt. Kimball was an influential friend of John P. Holland, the founder of the company that would
become Lake's chief nemesis when he attempted to interest the government in his submarine designs.[14]

The government's first announcement, in 1888, requesting experimental submarine designs for the competition was concise yet intentionally
vague because of the lack of knowledge concerning underwater navigation. The guidelines stressed eight requirements:

1. Safety.
2. Facility and certainty of action when submerged (ability to circle in
   a space no greater than four times the submarine length).
3. Speed when running on the surface (15 knots). The main engine
   should be capable of generating 1,000 horsepower.
4. Speed when submerged (8 knots).

5. Endurance, both submerged and on the surface (2 hours submerged at 8 knots with provision for 90 hours).
6. Offensive power (torpedoes with 100-pound charges of gun cotton).
7. Stability (positive buoyancy at all times).
8. Visibility of the object to be attacked.[15]

Congress had appropriated $200,000 for the construction of submarine boats. In reply to the navy's first announcement for the competition, four inventors submitted their plans: John Holland of New Jersey, Thorsten Nordenfelt of Sweden, George Baker of Chicago, and Josiah H. L. Tuck of New York.[16] Later that year it was announced that John Holland had won the competition. However, because of nonconformity in the bid, the contract was not awarded. Apparently, the Cramp Shipbuilding Company of Philadelphia (through which Holland had submitted his plans) had made no deposit nor provided any guarantee of operation as was required under the appropriation. Holland had won the competition but lost the contract. The funding was used for other naval building projects.[17]

The next year, 1889, a second competition was announced, and Holland was to win this one as well. However, President Cleveland lost his reelection bid to William H. Harrison, who installed General Benjamin F. Tracy as the new secretary of the navy, and Tracy quickly reassigned the submarine allocation to the completion of surface vessels then under construction.[18] Discouraged, Holland put away his submarine plans and turned his energies to the development of an airplane. His comments concerning this period of his life, which probably reflected the feeling of the other competitors concerning the Navy Department's handling of competitions, were summed up as follows: "This long delay was owing to the opposition of a few officers of conservative spirit who would prefer to see the value of the submarine boats fully established by their employment in other navies and their place in schemes of attack and defense properly located before they could recommend their adoption in our own navy."[19] Holland went on to say, "I was totally sick and disgusted with its [the Navy Department's] action, and was seriously tempted to abandon all further attempts to convince and awake it from its lethargy."[20]

In 1892 Grover Cleveland was returned to the White House as president, and on March 3, 1893, another congressional allocation for $200,000 was at hand for the reopening of the competition for submarines. This time, Simon Lake would be one of three contenders for the government's call.

George F. Baker of Chicago again submitted his design (in actuality, two designs that were similar except for the shape of the hull). The proposed craft was to be sixty feet in length, with a 120-ton displacement. Her expected speed was seven knots (approximately eight miles per hour). The submarine was to be propelled by the combination of a steam engine for surface running and electric motors while submerged. Ingeniously, Baker was the first to suggest that the electric motors be clutched to the steam engine, which would permit the electric motors to serve as dynamos (i.e., generators) and charge the accumulators (i.e., batteries) while the craft cruised under steam when awash. In other words, the submarine did not have to return to shore to recharge its batteries. The use of steam to drive a submarine, however, still was not very practical because, as discussed above, the high temperatures within the craft would be overwhelming to the crew. Further, the time required to prepare the boat for diving was prolonged, thereby increasing the craft's vulnerability to enemy ships. It should be noted, however, that steam power was employed in submarines well into the second decade of the twentieth century, especially by the British.[21]

The second competitor to submit plans was John P. Holland. Convinced by E. B. Frost (the man who would become the founder of the Electric Boat Company) that he must reenter the fray of submarine construction, Holland ferreted out his old plans. These called for a craft 85 feet in length with an 11 1/2-foot diameter and a 168-ton submerged displacement. The method for the control of its porpoiselike dive pattern was a set of vertical and horizontal rudders in the rear of the craft. The sub was to be propelled by triple screws operated by three independent sets of triple-expansion steam engines. Supposedly, it would develop 1,625 horsepower and be able to reach "guaranteed" speeds of fifteen knots on the surface, fourteen knots awash, and eight knots when submerged. This submarine was to have an endurance of twelve hours at full speed and a radius of action of one thousand miles if operated at lower speeds. She would be able to remain submerged for ten hours and run at six knots. Holland was proposing to use electric motors and storage batteries for underwater running. By this time, advancements had been made in the construction of more powerful electric motors and reliable batteries, and Holland believed he could use these motors, said to be capable of generating 70 horsepower. The sub would be able to discharge five Whitehead torpedoes from two expulsion tubes. These were very generous pronouncements for a submarine, considering the primitive state of propulsive systems and the general lack of information regarding underwater navigation at this point in history. As will be discussed later, this submarine, the

Plunger, was actually being built when Holland gave up, recognizing that the craft was a failure and could not meet the grandiose speculations made for it.[22] Holland would begin work on the now famous *Holland,* which was destined to become the U.S. Navy's first submarine.

Lake's submission to this submarine competition was a craft measuring eighty-five feet in length and also equipped with oil-burning boilers to run triple-expansion steam engines. Shortly after his submission, Lake recognized the foolhardiness of employing steam engines in submarines and would replace them with internal combustion engines. He would be one of the first to use this type of engine as the sole driving force to propel a submarine over long distances both above and below the surface, initially employing a long, snorkel-like hose to supply air to the engine. Lake included his characteristic wheels and his diving chamber, which he thought useful in military submarines for planting mines or cutting communication cables. Fore and aft hydroplanes, which permitted his submarine to descend on an even keel rather than diving to the bottom, were also prominent features of his design. He added still another innovation that was to become standard even in latter-day submarines: double-hull construction. The double hull provided space to house the gasoline tanks, thereby reducing the danger of carrying this volatile and explosive fuel within the submarine.[23] Lake had paid meticulous attention to the navy's requirements set forth in the 1888 competition for submarines, noting particularly the need for safety.

The differences between the Lake and Holland submarines were at once obvious. Holland wanted a fast attack submarine that would operate on a hit-and-run basis. Lake's craft was primarily designed for coastal defense and incorporated many of the components he employed in his salvage submarines (e.g., wheels, diving chamber, hydroplanes for even-keel diving). Lake's submission was basically a diving platform from which various activities such as mine planting and cable cutting could be undertaken. His submarine was more a defensive than an offensive weapon.

Lake went to the office of the secretary of the navy in June of 1893 to submit his plans. He was surprised to find the anteroom filled by a crowd of people. Taking a seat, he was joined by a talkative young man who inquired whether he was present to bid for the navy's submarine contract. Lake answered in the affirmative and then asked if all of the other individuals in the room were doing likewise. The answer he received shocked him. Only two others, John Holland, who was standing on the far side of the room, and the young man's father, George F. Baker, were there to submit their plans. The majority of the crowd were senators, former congress-

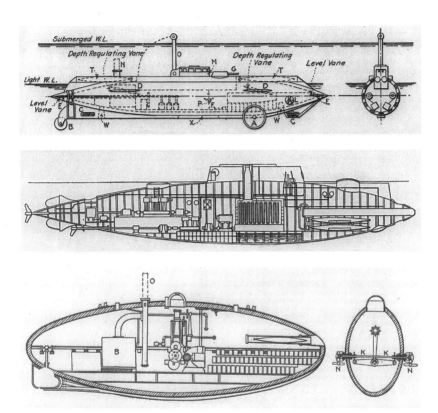

fig. 5. Submarine designs by Lake (*top*), Holland (*middle*), and Baker (*bottom*) submitted to the 1893 Navy Department during the 1893 competition. Courtesy J. B. Lippencott Company

men, and lawyers who apparently had come to lobby for the two main contenders, Baker and Holland.[24] Lake would long remember this day. "After a time," he recalled, "I was permitted to submit my plans. No one seemed to be at all interested in them or me. No one wanted to talk to me or ask questions. Later I was to learn that inventors are not highly regarded in government offices."[25]

After submitting his plans, Lake returned home to Baltimore. Shortly thereafter, he received a telegram from the editor of the *New York Tribune* telling him that his plans had been looked upon very favorably by the majority of the naval board judging the submissions. The newsman's congratulatory remarks, however, were premature, for during the following weeks Lake learned that the navy had again decided not to build any submarines.[26]

What occurred during the summer of 1893 is shrouded in mystery, and various sources have provided as many descriptions. Apparently, Baker's influence in Washington was substantial, and it was rumored at the time that he fully expected to win the competition. He had, in fact, moved from Chicago to Washington preparatory to the final announcement. Unfortunately, during this interval, he died. Baker had completed construction of his submarine, which was based at Lake Erie, and was prepared to demonstrate this submarine to the naval board. Meanwhile, E. B. Frost, now committed to the newly formed Holland Torpedo Boat Company, began a series of political and business transactions that were to become legendary in the halls of Washington. First, he convinced John Holland that he needed to build his submarine and then proceeded to generate the funding for this endeavor. Next, he initiated talks with representatives from Baker's company about the possibility of joining forces in exchange for $200,000 in Holland Company stock. Before any agreement had been established, Frost sent these stocks to Baker's lawyer for "services or services to be rendered." This was premature on Frost's part because the Baker people had no intention of relinquishing what they thought was their edge on the competition. Frost would later apologize for this error in judgment, claiming that he was unaware that the Baker company was still a client of the lawyer to whom he had sent the stocks. The Holland-Baker union would never occur.[27]

Frost's final gambit must have involved a serious amount of wheeling and dealing with naval and governmental officials. He sought a congressional resolution to prevent the appropriated funds from being diverted away from submarine construction. The result of this maneuvering would ultimately lead to a major exposé of political influence peddling in Washington. Frost registered a series of Holland patents abroad and empowered his foreign representatives to negotiate contracts with interested governments. This was an obvious ploy to force the U.S. government into constructing the Holland submarine because inserted in the contracts was the stipulation that no construction could be undertaken until one year after the Holland submarine was built for the U.S. government. This move was to create problems for John Holland some five years later when these patent registrations were subjected to a hearing by the House Committee on Naval Affairs. However, the Holland Company's dealings with foreign governments apparently did prod the U.S. government into action, for on March 3, 1895, Frost received the $200,000 submarine contract. Thus, the Holland Torpedo Boat Company would begin work on its first submarine, the *Plunger*. Meanwhile, Simon Lake had distanced himself from the events occurring in the nation's capital in order to consider the possibility of building his submarine with private funding.[28]

Lake had been running a successful business in Baltimore, manufacturing a winding gear for commercial oyster boats. This winding gear was the first mechanism he had designed and patented. It would be the first of over two hundred patents he would eventually hold. Excited at the possibility of building a submarine, he left his father and wife in charge of the Baltimore business and moved to New York, where he opened an office in the old Cheeseborough Building for the purpose of securing funds to build his salvaging submarine *Argonaut.* After spending six months and all of his savings, he had not raised a single dollar. Lake thought that an endorsement by a renowned engineer might provide an incentive to investors, so he approached Charles H. Haswell, the former chief engineer of the U.S. Navy, to view his plans. Haswell agreed, for a fee of fifteen hundred dollars. Lake's mouth dropped open; he did not have fifteen dollars, let alone a hundred times that sum. Haswell must have recognized that Lake was unable to pay for the endorsement, but recognizing the frustrations of the young inventor, he offered to "look it over and give you a report anyhow, and you can repay me at some future time when you are able."[29] Lake was elated, but the elation was to be short-lived for even with Haswell's endorsement he was still unable to induce anyone to invest in his dream. It was at this point that he scaled down his plans and returned to the Atlantic Highlands of New Jersey to build the prototype *Argonaut Junior,* using his own limited resources and funding provided by family members.

The *Junior's* public demonstration in 1893 was successful and served to generate the financial interest Lake had hoped it would. As with many promising inventions, several promoters now made their appearance on the scene. One individual in particular claimed to be a friend of the Vanderbilts, Astors, and Goulds and, as such, was certain that these wealthy families would subscribe to Lake Company stock. The promoter attempted to convince Lake that he should be given sole control of the company's finances and stock sales. A rather convoluted situation developed, the outcome of which was that Lake came very close to being swindled. Lake would almost certainly have gone to jail had it not been for a nagging intuition and advice from trusted friends. Fortunately, the Lake Submarine Company was saved and, thanks to a large number of honest small investors, Lake was able to raise sufficient capital to lay plans for the construction of the "mother" to the *Argonaut Junior,* which Lake would christen the *Argonaut.*[30]

By 1895, Lake was ready to begin construction of the *Argonaut* and signed a contract with the Columbian Iron Works and Dry Dock Company in Baltimore, where she was to be built. Ironically, this was the same company selected by the Holland Company to build the *Plunger,* the boat that was supposed to be the navy's first submarine. Both submarines would be launched in 1897 and go into dry dock together that year for finishing. The *Argonaut* would make numerous test dives and go on to salvage a multitude of cargoes from various wrecks in Long Island Sound, making Simon Lake a wealthy man. Holland's *Plunger* would be abandoned.[31]

CHAPTER 2

A Craft with a Long History

In the ocean depths off Madagascar, obsolete fish keep their laggard appointments. In the depths of the human mind, obsolete assumptions go their daily rounds. And there is little difference between the two, except that fish do no harm.

—*Robert Ardrey, African Genesis*

Simon Lake did not invent the submarine. He, like most inventors, relied upon the successes and failures of his forebears. The name of the person who first ventured below the surface of the water in some type of primitive submarine or diving device has in all likelihood been lost in the miasmal mist of prehistory. Further, the sparse, often inaccurate records of ancient nautical history provide only a fleeting glimpse into the exploits of those adventurers who made the preliminary attempts to penetrate this primeval environment. The period between the sixteenth and twentieth centuries, however, affords increasingly accurate documentation of efforts to develop the technologies necessary to conquer this environment. It is rife with both successful and failed attempts that laid the foundation for present-day underwater endeavors. One thing is clear: the driving force stimulating submarine development has been militaristic. Alex Roland has painted a remarkable picture of the rationale behind the development of underwater warfare during the age of sail.[1] Large, powerful navies were viewed as Goliaths, while nations having weaker naval strength considered submarines the Davids that could destroy an enemy fleet unawares from the depths of the ocean. The submarine represented potential naval power, but like many inventions, its development had to await the concomitant technological developments that would make underwater warfare feasible. Further, and of equal significance, military acceptance of the submarine as a weapon was slow in coming. Dastardly sneak attacks from below the water's surface did not fit the established "chivalry" of warfare. The submarine would assist in changing attitudes toward fairness in battle.

Archaeological studies have provided evidence that early humans have been diving into the sea to retrieve its bounty since at least 7000 B.C. Ancient literature and artwork from Thebes in Greece (ca. 3200 B.C.) suggest involvement in various types of underwater activity. The artifacts of the seafaring culture that existed on the island of Crete around 2250 B.C. have provided evidence that divers were part of a major industry that collected sponges for household and commercial purposes. The ancient Greeks and Romans were so tied to the sea that they apparently found it necessary to have a god-protector for those who went below its surface. Glaucus was (and is today) the Greek patron saint of divers. In the nineteenth century B.C., Homer chronicled the exploits of divers in his *Iliad,* and in the fifth century B.C. Herodotus described how Scyllias, a warrior in the Median Wars, was able to swim eighty stadia (about nine miles) underwater without surfacing. No description of how he accomplished this feat was provided.[2]

The first and probably best known submarine (more likely, diving bell) is the underwater craft of Alexander the Great (356–323 B.C.). As with much of ancient history, there are several different versions of how Alexander accomplished his deep-sea visitations. The craft has been variously described as a glass barrel or wooden barrel (the latter covered with asses' skins and equipped with small portholes and a water-tight door). This crude device was said to measure ten cubits long by five cubits wide (approximately four by sixteen feet) and was moved along the harbor bottom by a gantry suspended between two ships. Alexander and two of his secretaries reportedly made several trips to the harbor bottom and returned each time with wild tales of the sea monsters they had seen.[3]

As the centuries progressed, many would-be submarine inventors designed and, in some cases, built craft that would permit them to go below the water's surface. Even the Renaissance genius Leonardo da Vinci is said to have drawn up plans for a crude submarine but quickly destroyed them, stating, "How and why I do not describe my method for remaining under water for as long a time as I can remain without food; and this I do not publish or divulge on account of the evil nature of men who practice assassination at the bottom of the sea."[4]

Numerous individuals would hypothesize and others would make actual attempts to gain entrance to Poseidon's kingdom with crude diving gear and diving bells, but it was Cornelius Van Drebbel in A.D. 1620 who actually succeeded in constructing a craft that was the forerunner of today's submarines.[5] This Dutch physician lived in England and managed to build a boat that was rowed both above and below the river Thames for a distance of about two miles. Van Drebbel may owe his inspiration to an Englishman named William Bourne, who in 1578 drew up plans for a craft that, in many respects, resembles the one constructed by Van Drebbel. Bourne, like many before him, probably did nothing more than design a submarine. However, he did provide a number of interesting features such as internal leather bags that would serve to take on ballast water for diving. These bags were emptied by large screw mechanisms that squeezed the water out when it was desirable to return to the surface. Air for breathing was obtained through a hollow mast. Bourne appears to have been the first to suggest double-hull construction, but his double hull was to be used for the containment of an air supply for the sub's crew, not for ballast water.[6]

Van Drebbel's craft was built of wood and rendered watertight by stretching greased leather over the hull. Ballast control was effected in the manner suggested by Bourne: leather "joints" were allowed to flood during a dive, and the water was squeezed out for surfacing. The submarine could operate at a depth of twelve to fifteen feet for several hours. The propulsion system consisted of oars fitted through the sides of the craft and externally sealed with flexible leather gaskets. Van Drebbel claims to have developed a secret elixir that purified the air within the craft and permitted him to remain submerged for extended periods of time. However, no one has ever been able to identify this elixir. During the next few years, he built two additional craft, the largest said to be capable of carrying twelve rowers besides his passengers. His intimate friend and supporter, King James I, is said to have made a lengthy trip with Van Drebbel. Unfortunately, this builder of the first submarine died in 1634, leaving behind no records of his experimental work. Our knowledge of his efforts is derived from various reports of the time.[7]

About this same time, two now long-forgotten French priests took an interest in submarine design and published a small work that envisioned many aspects of the submarines to come. Fathers Mersenne and Fournier were the first to propose that submarines be composed of metal having a pisciform shape. They also suggested the use of wheels to propel the vessel over the sea bottom but maintained the characteristic propulsion system of the day, oars. They were well ahead of their time in their incorporation of air pumps, a primitive periscope, and a simple escape hatch. Further, the craft was to be armed with a cannon to blow an enemy to oblivion, a rather strange suggestion from two priests. Reference to a portion of their monograph survives today in a unique spot in world literature: in discussing underwater phenomena, the two priests mentioned a Sicilian swimmer named Nicholas who could travel long distances underwater with a single breath; the swimmer's name appears as "Colas the Fish" in Miguel de Cervantes's 1605 novel *Don Quixote*.[8]

Diving bells seemed to have become a craze during the seventeenth century, and a number were built and used primarily for salvaging operations. Of particular note is the one constructed by Sir Edmond Halley (1656–1742), the multitalented scientist known today for the comet that bears his name. His device was bucket shaped, measuring five to six feet in diameter at its base, which remained open to permit direct access to the ocean bottom. It was constructed of wood with lead sheathing on its exterior. Several glass viewing ports provided some light and allowed for limited lateral observation. Additional ballast weights were hung with ropes to the outer perimeter (apparently predating the use of a drop keel). With three occupants on board, the bell would be lowered into the ocean by a ship's boom. They could remain underwater for almost two hours at ten fathoms. A unique aspect of Halley's craft was the renewal of air within the bell by using wooden casks drawn down from its mother ship. Water pressure was used to force the air out of the casks and into the bell, while spent air was released from cocks at the top of the diving bell. All indications are that Halley's device was successfully employed for the shallow-water salvaging of cannon and other artifacts lost with sunken ships.[9]

The eighteenth and nineteenth centuries witnessed many additions to and refinements in submarine technology, particularly in Europe. However, an increasing number of submarines built by Americans would markedly alter submarine history and underwater navigation. The first appeared during the American Revolution and was constructed by David Bushnell at Old Lyme, Connecticut. Coincidentally, Old Lyme is a short distance from the location that was destined to become the U.S. Submarine Base at New London in 1916. Bushnell's craft is now recognized as the first submarine to operate under battle conditions and to give "incontestably valuable results."[10]

Bushnell's invention was dubbed the *Turtle* because its shape resembled a chelonian shell standing on end. Its configuration was designed not for speed but for stealth. The craft was built in three months and

clearly demonstrated an ample amount of Yankee ingenuity. The top of
the submarine supported a small conning tower with its water-tight hatch
and small portholes for sighting enemy ships when running awash. The
single operator had only the contained air for breathing, which would last
approximately one half hour while propelling the sub underwater. It may
have been the first submarine to bear snorkles for supplying air when the
conning tower was above water level. The *Turtle* was kept upright by lead
ballast at its bottom, the lead weight being releasable should the craft encounter difficulties. Internal ballast tanks were flooded by opening stop-
cocks. A pump permitted the operator to "blow" the tanks and surface.
Steering was accomplished by a rudder in the rear. The craft's method of
propulsion has been a topic of discussion among submarine enthusiasts
for many years. Bushnell describes oars, but difficulties with interpreting
his style of writing have caused others to suggest that he actually used
screw propellers turned by an internal crank.[11] In point of fact, he describes the use of two devices of the same configuration, one for propulsion and the other for the control of vertical position. It is difficult to
visualize how an oar could accomplish the latter but rather easy to envision a vertical screw to raise and lower the craft. An objection to the no-
tion that he used a screw propeller stems from what was thought to be
the definitive record of its invention sometime after 1800. However, recent
findings indicate that in 1680 the famed biologist Robert Hooke actually
described a "screw to work water." Additionally, it should be recalled that
the Archimedian Screw, circa 200 B.C., predated both Hooke and Bushnell.
Bushnell had been a student at Yale University and had access to the information contained in the university's library, which, in all likelihood, contained Hooke's studies.

Another bit of Bushnell's ingenuity was the depth gauge he incorporated into the *Turtle*. His submarine had been designed to operate under
the cover of darkness. The small portholes in the conning tower hardly
permitted sunlight to enter the interior, let alone moonlight. It would
therefore be impossible for the operator to read the depth gauge, which
was a manometer (i.e., a closed glass tube opening to the exterior of the
craft). Bushnell solved the problem by placing a piece of cork coated with
foxfire within the glass tube. Foxfire is the luminescent fungus common
to marshy areas of New England. It commonly emits an eerie green glow
after rain storms. In a similar fashion, he used foxfire to illuminate his
compass. This primitive lighting system was partially responsible for de-
termining when the submarine could be used. Bushnell had originally
planned to attack the British fleet in late fall of 1775, but an early frost

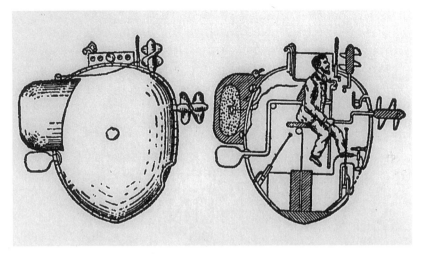

fig. 6. David Bushnell's *Turtle*. Courtesy J. B. Lippencott Company

put an end to his supply of foxfire, which some say forced him to sit out the winter.[12]

Bushnell's armament for his tiny submarine consisted of a mine carried behind the conning tower and containing 150 pounds of powder. Attaching the mine to an enemy vessel was tricky at best, but his method was ingenious for its time. He planned to approach an enemy ship at night with only the conning tower exposed. Upon reaching a position close to the vessel but still unseen by it, the operator would submerge, cruising the remaining distance underwater. Once under the ship, he would pump out sufficient ballast water to bring the conning tower into contact with the ship's hull. Positioned on the conning tower was an auger that could be turned from inside the submarine. The bit was attached to the mine by a ring and a short chain. The operator would drill into the hull and then drive the submarine forward, snapping the bit off and leaving the mine attached to its prey. Some reports indicate that a clock mechanism inside the mine would be activated as the sub pulled away. Others have suggested that a flintlock mechanism would be triggered by pulling on a long cord paid out from the submarine, detonating the mine and sending its victim to the bottom. According to one historian, this craft may have been inspected and evaluated by none other than Benjamin Franklin, who recommended its use to George Washington.[13]

As with many inventions, what works on paper often has a way of malfunctioning when put into practice. The rumblings of revolution in

1775 had caused the British to send a fleet of ships to blockade the areas in and around New York City. Bushnell was given permission by Generals George Washington and Samuel Holden Parsons to mount an attack on the sixty-four-gun flagship, *HMS Eagle,* anchored north of Staten Island, New York. The *Turtle* was towed from Old Lyme to Falkner's Island and then to Charles Island in Long Island Sound. Finally, she was moved to New Rochelle, New York, and then transported overland to the Hudson River. Preparations were made at Whitehall Steps near the tip of Manhattan for the first attack. But things immediately began to go awry.

The operator of the *Turtle,* who had been with Bushnell from her inception, reported sick. His replacement was a rather nervous army sergeant named Ezra Lee. Lee set out against the *Eagle* with minimal instruction. The craft was towed into the waters near Governor's Island and released. Lee was now on his own. He could see the silhouette of the massive frigate in the moonlight as he began turning the crank that would deliver him to his destiny. The *Turtle* approached the *Eagle* undetected and submerged at its stern. Pumping water out of the ballast tank, Lee heard a thump and recognized that he was under his target. He began turning the auger but found that it would not bite into the ship's hull. Some say that he had struck the iron bands supporting the rudder. Others believe that the *Eagle* had been one of the first British ships sheathed in copper. Whatever the case, Lee was unable to attach the mine. Acutely aware that his air was being exhausted, he decided it was time for retreat. A short distance from the frigate, Lee adjusted his ballast, permitting the sub's conning tower to break the surface, where he was able to renew his air supply. Daylight was fast approaching, and the tide had shifted, drawing him relentlessly into the midst of the British fleet. Just as Lee was thinking that things had reached their lowest ebb, he heard the shouts of British sailors in the picket boats guarding the fleet. He had been spotted. As would become the standard defensive maneuver of all submariners to follow in his wake, Lee slammed shut the hatch and dove. He released the mine in open water, which reduced the drag on the *Turtle,* making his struggle with the changing tide easier to deal with. He laboriously drove the submarine toward the shore. There was a loud explosion, and a huge column of water rose skyward. Frantically, the British longboats searched the area. Lee, meanwhile, was able to make it back to shore.

Bushnell and Lee thus became the first to launch a submarine into battle and attack an enemy surface vessel. Although no ship was sunk, nor were any of the enemy killed or wounded, in failure they found success because the British fleet was ordered out of New York. The city had been saved from invasion. The *Turtle* was never used again, and it's doubtful that Ezra Lee ever would have reentered what he must have thought would be his coffin.

David Bushnell would make another attempt to sink the King's Navy in December of 1777. He set loose kegs of powder rigged as contact mines in the Delaware River above a mooring area where several British ships were anchored. Again, problems with the tide and water currents caused the kegs to go astray, but one did manage to blow up a boatload of British sailors investigating these strange contraptions. This little event in history was memorialized in a Revolutionary ballad appropriately entitled "The Battle of the Kegs."[14] Shortly after his attack, Bushnell was arrested by the British and then released as a "harmless country clod."[15] After the war, he moved to Georgia and changed his name to Dr. Bush. Some believe that this name change was the result of the public animosity toward anyone involved with "villainous submersibles." Bushnell would live to the ripe old age of ninety but would die in obscurity, never being formally recognized by his government for his contributions.[16]

The name Robert Fulton conjures in the minds of most people images of the steamboat *Clermont* churning its way up the Hudson River. Few realize that this inventive American also built submarines. The concept of the submarine was not novel when Fulton began designing his *Nautilus* in France in 1797. His cherished ambition in life had been to become a great constructor of canals, but his phenomenal engineering abilities, coupled with an insatiable curiosity, led him to consider the viability of underwater travel. Like that of many of his contemporaries, part of his inspiration for building a submarine lay with a desire for "lessening the power of the English fleet"[17] and his "sympathy with the ideals of the French Revolution."[18] However, Fulton has been described as an egotist with a good business sense, more concerned with capitalism than patriotism. "When the French declined his offer to blow up the English, he went to the English and offered to blow up the French, meanwhile doing business with both."[19]

Fulton's submarine endeavors began in 1799 when he received permission to build his *Nautilus* from none other than First Consul Napoleon Bonaparte. With a grant of ten thousand francs, Fulton set about building his submarine. The craft had the shape of an imperfect ellipsoid, twenty-one feet in length and six feet at its broadest point. A thick, hollow iron keel extended the length of the submarine, serving as both a guide and a ballast tank. According to Fulton's calculations, the volume of the hollow keel could be adjusted so accurately with the pumps he used that the difference between the weight of flotation and the water displaced by it was four to five kilograms. The top of the submarine sported a dome-shaped conning tower with a hatch and small portholes of glass. As with Bushnell's craft, propulsion was accomplished by a hand-cranked screw propeller placed ahead of a rudder. One of the unique features of Fulton's *Nautilus* that exemplifies the propulsion problem plaguing submarines of the time was a fan-shaped sail used to propel the craft on the surface. This unit was folded down and stowed prior to diving. A three-man crew was needed to operate this craft.[20]

Fulton's submarine bore a spar torpedo of rather strange design. A spar torpedo is a gunpowder mine attached to the bowsprit of a craft and rammed into its target during battle. It was a dangerous arrangement because the mine's explosion had the potential to sink the craft delivering the weapon. Fulton modified this design by using a hollow spar containing a rod sharpened at its attacking end and attached in the rear to the mine. Once the rod was driven into the enemy's hull, the submarine could back off, leaving the mine attached to the ship. From a safe distance, he could detonate the mine by pulling on a long cord paid out from the submarine and activating its firing device.[21]

On July 24, 1800, the *Nautilus* was launched in Brest harbor and made its first dive, plunging to a depth of twenty-five feet and remaining there for five minutes. Encountering difficulties with the currents, Fulton halted the test after the second dive, which lasted seventeen minutes. At La Havre in late November he resumed his tests and was able to remain submerged for six hours. He was able to attain a speed of one knot (about 0.9 mph) with his two crew members operating the crank. After these initial trials, Fulton was given an audience with Napoleon. The future emperor of France appears to have been impressed and turned the matter over to Admiral Denis Decrès, minister of marine, for further evaluation. While awaiting a reply from the emperor, Fulton penned the following in a letter: "You will permit me to observe that although I have the highest respect for you and the other members of the Government, and although I retain the most ardent desire to see the English Government beaten, never the less the cold and discouraging manner with which all my exertions have been treated during the past three years will compel me to abandon the enterprise in France if I am not received in a more friendly and liberal manner."[22]

In an attempt to further influence Napoleon, Fulton arranged a demonstration of the offensive capability of his submarine with Admiral Jean Vellaret. On 23d Thermidor (the eleventh month of the French Revolutionary calendar) a forty-foot sloop was anchored in the harbor, and Fulton attacked with a "bomb" (i.e., a mine attached to his spar torpedo apparatus) containing twenty pounds of powder. In Fulton's own words, the sloop was "torn into Atoms, in fact nothing was left but the buye and cable, And the concussion was so great that a Column of Water Smoak and fibers of the Sloop was cast 80 to 100 feet in the Air, this Simple Experiment at once Proved the effect of the Bomb Submarine to the Satisfaction of all the Spectators."[23]

Fulton's enthusiasm for his success was elevated when in September of 1801 he received notification that Napoleon himself wanted to inspect the submarine. However, this was prevented by the fact that Fulton, in his dismay with the French government's lack of immediate interest, had destroyed the *Nautilus*. His impetuous action and poor judgment had sealed his fate with Napoleon. The emperor was said to have regarded Fulton as a "charlatan and swindler, intent only on extorting money."[24]

Parsons has described Fulton as a "radical republican, hating all forms of autocracy."[25] As Napoleon approached the status of an undeclared dictator, Fulton felt ethically free to approach the British government, which, through its secret service, was aware of the French experiments with the *Nautilus*. Fulton was of the opinion that Napoleon had set himself above all law when, in 1802, he made himself consul for life and, in 1804, proclaimed himself emperor. Apparently, Fulton's approach to Britain was unnecessary, as the autumn of 1803 brought with it a request to build submarines for England. Submitting a description of updated plans (which he had kept secret from the French), Fulton provided a listing of his needs and a request for one hundred thousand pounds. The funding was reduced to forty thousand pounds but proved sufficient to reinstitute Fulton's submarine endeavors.

By 1805, Fulton had submitted to the British Admiralty his refined plans for a submarine based upon his experiences with the *Nautilus*. He built his second submarine during this period, his first for the British government. The craft was, by all accounts, a semisubmersible catamaran equipped with a time bomb. The operator paddled the partially submerged vessel to an enemy ship and, after attaching it, swam away to safety. Apparently, Fulton's device was used against the French fleet at Boulogne, but the attack proved a failure. The French, ironically, branded the British cowards and beasts who demonstrated unchivalrous behavior.

Fulton was able to destroy the brig *Dorothea* with this device on October 15 in the presence of Prime Minister William Pitt and other officials. It was a feat that raised Fulton's optimism for his submersible. Six days

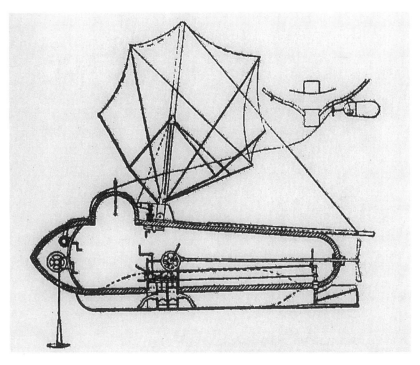

fig. 7. Robert Fulton's *Nautilus* (courtesy J. B. Lippencott Company) and Halstead's *Intelligent Whale* (courtesy Naval Historical Center)

later, however, Fulton's hopes and dreams were dashed after Lord Nelson destroyed the combined French and Spanish fleet at Trafalgar. England no longer needed submarines, as its ships were now supreme rulers of the global waters.[26]

The *Nautilus* represented a significant contribution to submarine construction. Fulton had clearly demonstrated that it possessed real offensive power. Further, even with all of its recognized defects, this submarine proved that controlled underwater travel was possible. Additionally, Fulton was able to demonstrate that the craft could remain submerged for several hours while maneuvering underwater by compass. Lacking any further British support for his experimentation, Fulton decided to return home. In a letter to Lord Castlereagh from London dated December 13, 1805,[27] he made his first reference to the possibility of approaching the American government with his submarine designs.

> I have now said sufficient of this System to enable any ingenious man to make and arrange the Engines and any maritime nation to carry the whole into effect. If I live it is my intention to give this system to the public engraved with every detail and I have made these sketches and this loose description which is little more than a sketch of my studies on the Subject. In order that they may not be lost to my country and mankind in case of any accident to me. The prosecution of this system will put maritime nations on equal means of offensive war, will give them equal means of distressing each others commerce or destroying their Ships of War and consequently will produce the liberty of the seas. . . . It may be necessary to give a reason for offering to abandon these inventions to the British government to use or not as they might think proper.
>
> My first reason is that my country does not at present seem to require such engines. And although I had written to Mr. Jefferson twice on the progress I had made and the final happy consequences of such a system I never had an answer from him nor do I know I shall have the least encouragement in America to systematize these plans for the use of the country.
>
> Second, Until my country feels the importance of these engines and seeing the power which they possess to give liberty of the seas, and will unite with me in introducing them effectually into the world, and considering the immense advantages which America would gain from a perfect liberty of the seas, . . . It is

right I Should do everything in my power for the interest of
such friends and even to guard my own Interest. Will any American or liberal minded man call such actions sorded and wish me
to abandon years of Industry to the public good while neither
he nor the government have offered me one Shilling to promote
so glorious an enterprise?[28]

Fulton returned to the United States in 1806 and did receive limited
monetary support from the government to continue his submarine work.
Eight years later, he completed the *Mute*, an eighty-one-foot-long monster
with a twenty-one-foot beam. It was driven by paddle wheels and manned
by a crew of a hundred men. Its large size proved to be its failing, and the
uncontrollable submarine was abandoned.[29] Fulton died in 1815, but during the last nine years of his life he left his most significant mark on history, the steamboat *Clermont.*

Before considering the American submarines constructed during the
Civil War, mention should be made here of three somewhat successful but
little-known submarines that have been largely overlooked by history.
They are important because they demonstrate a developing interest in underwater warfare in the United States, probably as the result of Fulton's
efforts combined with the numerous submarine innovations arising in
Europe during this period. In 1862 the U.S. government requested that a
Frenchman named M. Villeroi build a cigar-shaped submarine measuring
thirty-five feet in length and three feet nine inches in diameter. She was
built in ten cylindrical sections with two conical end sections. She had
lateral and horizontal planes fitted to the last three sections of the craft to
control its stability, a forerunner to Lake's hydroplanes. The first run of
this craft lasted about two hours, with most of this time spent cruising
below the surface at sixteen to twenty feet. According to the only account
of this submarine, she was very maneuverable and had a diver's chamber
that permitted collection of materials from the bottom. Unfortunately,
nothing more is known about Villeroi's submarine.[30]

The second of the unknown American submarines is controversial.
Because she purportedly had the distinction of being first to use a mixed
propulsion system (steam and electricity), some authorities question her
existence.[31] An engineer named Alstitt supposedly built this craft for the
U.S. government in Mobile, Alabama, in 1863. This large submarine was
divided into two decks. The upper one contained the steam engines, operating machinery, and armament, while the lower deck housed the fore
and aft ballast tanks with a coal bunker in between. A small conning tower

similar to the one on Fulton's *Nautilus* was located amidships and provided access to the interior. Diving this submarine required a good deal
of time. The smokestack from the boiler had to be retracted and covered
while the fires used to generate the steam had to be put out. Excess steam
pressure had to be released. The electric motor then had to be geared to
the propeller. A rather peculiar diving plane or rudder placed at the bow
of the craft was used to force it underwater. The armament consisted of
mines carried along the sides of the craft that were to be laid down in the
vicinity of an enemy vessel and detonated by an electric spark carried by
wire from the submarine. As with Villeroi's submarine, history has lost
track of her performance and fate.[32]

Almost two decades before the above two submarines were built, a
shoemaker named Loder Phillips conceived and built a number of submarines, some of which were launched and used in Lake Michigan. His first
submarine was built in Michigan City about 1845. The descriptions of the
craft are sparse, but she apparently sank in twelve feet of water during
trials. She was later raised and modified. No loss of life occurred. Shortly
afterward, Phillips built another craft that met the same fate, sinking in
the Chicago river. She was found and raised in 1915 as part of a salvaging
operation and placed on exhibition, where she was referred to as the *Fool
Killer*. According to reports of the time, Phillips had sold the submarine
to an easterner who disappeared in her. When the sub was found and
raised, she contained the bones of a man and his dog.[33]

Phillips's next attempt was more successful. The craft was cigar-shaped,
forty feet long and four feet wide. Apparently, she was safer than his previous submarines. Reports of the time state that he was able to take his wife
and two children with him to spend a day exploring the lake's bottom.
Further, he was able to fire a six-pound gun underwater, successfully sinking a target vessel. Phillips is also said to have developed an air purification
system rather than carrying compressed air for breathing, but no record
of this device has survived. The submarine could reach speeds of about
four knots when two men were cranking the double-bladed propeller. At
this point, the historical record becomes somewhat fuzzy. This submarine
or possibly a fourth model was reported as being lost after she began to
leak at a depth of one hundred feet. Returning to the surface, Phillips was
able to escape, but the sub was lost. His work on submarines continued,
and in 1862 he submitted plans to Gideon Wells, secretary of the navy, for a
craft specifically designed to sink the Confederate *Merrimack*. No further
records of the navy's action with respect to Phillips's efforts are available.[34]

The American Civil War marked a turning point in submarine history. The North had both a large number of ships and shipbuilding facilities that were successful in blockading the Confederacy. In an attempt to counter this naval superiority, the South retaliated with submersibles collectively called "*Davids*"—small, armed craft that would go out to slay the larger Philistine "Goliaths."

Many naval historians distinguish between the terms *submarine* and *submersible*. The former was considered to be a craft capable of operating equally well in both the submerged or partially submerged condition, while the latter was a compromised craft that remained partially submerged, never going fully below the surface.[35] Today, in light of the atomic submarines, the term *submarine* refers to a craft that does not have to surface to renew its air supply or its recharge batteries. Many of the early *Davids* were submersibles, being nothing more than low-riding boats armed with a spar torpedo.

Initial reports of the activities of these craft are sketchy, but during the evening of October 5, 1863, the Union ship *New Ironsides* was attacked near Charleston Harbor and almost sunk by a Confederate submersible. The postwar account of this attack provides a stark picture of this encounter. The Confederate craft was commanded by a Lieutenant Glasswell. The *David* involved in this attack was reported to be fifty feet in length, nine feet at her beam, and propelled by steam. Her low profile, coupled with the dark of night, permitted the submersible to approach her quarry in an awash condition. The captain of the submersible then proposed to reduce her speed to prevent sparks from the boiler's fires being detected against the evening skies. Her iron-pointed spar torpedo was to be rammed into the *New Ironsides*'s hull. The sub would then back off and the charge would be set off by pulling on a one hundred–foot line connected to the mine's firing mechanism. The explosion would deliver a concussive blow that would sink the Yankee vessel—at least that was the plan. The *David*, however, was spotted before reaching an attack position, and the Union crew began firing with both cannon and rifles. A bullet struck the spar torpedo, and a resounding explosion sent tons of water into the air. The *New Ironsides* rolled in response, while the *David* was lifted out of the water. The *David* came crashing to the surface and gave the impression that she was sinking. Glasswell led the crew as they abandoned the submersible. Realizing that she was still afloat and operational, the chief engineer and another crew member reboarded her and returned the *David* to the safety of Charleston Harbor. Lieutenant Glasswell and the other members of the crew were taken prisoners. The *New Ironsides* suffered only minor damage, but the attack caused major concern among Union naval officials.[36]

The most famous of the Confederate *Davids* was the *Hunley,* variously and disparagingly nicknamed the *Iron Witch,* the *Fish,* and the *Tin Coffin.* This notorious submarine was the brainchild of retired navy captain Horace L. Hunley, a naval hero, inventor, and gentleman cotton merchant of the Old South. Assisting him in this endeavor during the summer of 1863 was army captain James McClintock. The submarine was constructed in Mobile, Alabama, from a twenty-foot section of iron boiler, 3 1/2 feet wide and 5 feet deep. Both ends were pointed and contained the ballast tanks, each operated by a crew member. Unfortunately, Hunley constructed these tanks with open tops that would spill over into the crew's area if the valves stuck or the craft encountered a rough sea. This may well have been Hunley's undoing. In the forward and aft sections of the craft were dangerously low (sixteen inches high) conning towers (referred to as manholes) equipped with glass viewing ports called bull's eyes. Running the length of the inside was a crankshaft. The crank was turned by six crew members and delivered its power to an aft propeller. The commanding officer sat in the bow, where he could direct the craft's course through the viewing ports or the open manhole. The submarine was controlled from the bow by a cabled wheel that operated the rear rudder and by levers that set the angles of crude bow planes. Primitive snorkles permitted fresh air to enter when the *Hunley* ran awash. Like that of the other *Davids* before her, the *Hunley's* armament consisted of a spar torpedo containing ninety pounds of gunpowder.[37]

Hunley built his submarine at Mobile, bearing all the costs of its construction. Part of his motivation may have been an announcement by General G. T. Beauregard, commander of the Charleston forces, offering a bounty of $100,000 for the destruction of the steam ironclad *Ironsides* and $50,000 for each monitor sunk. However, Hunley was wealthy enough not to need such bounties, and it is more reasonable to attribute his efforts to his patriotism for the Confederacy.

The first mission was a harbinger of disaster. Entering Mobile Bay on her maiden voyage, the sub dove for the bottom, killing her crew of seven. Stuck in mud and refusing to budge, she was finally raised only with considerable effort. The *Hunley* was transported to Charleston on two railroad flat cars. A second crew, volunteers from the CSS *Chicora,* began training. Lieutenant John A. Payne commanded the craft. His shipmate from the *Chicora,* Lieutenant C. L. Stanton, was scheduled to be a member

fig. 8. The Confederate submarine *Hunley* as she appeared in dry dock. Courtesy Naval Historical Center

of the crew, but he arrived in Charleston after the sub sailed. Lieutenant Charles H. Hooker replaced Stanton. On August 23, 1863, the *Hunley* went out into Charleston Harbor from Sullivan's Island. An unrecorded accident forced her back for repairs. Then, on August 29, the submarine became entangled in ropes holding her to the steamer *Etiwan*. As the steamer moved away from the dock at Fort Johnson, she pulled the *Hunley* under the dock. Lt. Payne, standing on her deck, jumped free. Hooker made it to the forward manhole and began to climb out. Water pressure slammed the hatch on his leg, and the *Hunley* dragged him to the bottom. Desperately struggling with the hatch, Hooker was able to free himself and swim to the surface to be rescued by one of the *Chicora's* longboats. The remaining five crew members drowned in five fathoms of water. Payne and Hooker swore never to enter the craft again.[38]

The submarine was raised and refitted and a third crew enlisted. This time, Hunley himself agreed to command the submarine. He was convinced that the previous sinkings had resulted from improper handling of his brainchild. On October 15, 1863, he steered the craft down the Stono River and into the harbor. On his command, the sub went to the bottom—and did not come up. Divers found the craft several days later in nine fathoms of water, its bow implanted in the bottom mud. Inside were the bodies of Hunley and his seven crew members.[39]

After this tragedy, General Beauregard refused to let the *Hunley* be used again. But his edict did not last long. First Lieutenant George E.

Dixon had worked closely with Hunley and was convinced that the submarine represented a viable way to break the Union blockade. Beauregard relented, permitting the submarine to go out again. It would be her last voyage.[40]

In the early evening of February 17, 1864, the *Hunley* cast off her moorings. Her bow sported a fifteen-foot spar torpedo. The attack was to be made in a semisubmerged condition as per the orders of General Beauregard. Unfortunately, the sea was smooth and it was a moonlit night. The officer of the deck on board the USS *Housatonic* spotted the *Hunley* at about one hundred yards. Captain Charles W. Pickering and his executive officer, Lieutenant Francis J. Higginson, shouted orders to the crew of the *Housatonic*. The shouts were in vain. Dixon drove the *Hunley's* spar amidships. The new Yankee corvette went to bottom in minutes, apparently taking the *Hunley* and her crew with her. Thus the *Iron Witch* became the first submarine to sink an enemy warship in battle.

Some years later, the Daughters of the Confederacy erected a granite monument at the Meeting Street entrance to the Battery in Charleston. On its bronze plaque are the names of only sixteen of the more than thirty men who died as members of the *Hunley's* crews.[41]

A footnote needs to be added to the *Hunley* saga. During January of 1995, a group of underwater archaeologists found the rusting hulk of the *Hunley*. This undertaking was a joint effort by the South Carolina Institute of Archaeology at the University of South Carolina and the National Underwater and Marine Agency of Austin, Texas. Using a magnetometer and side-scan radar, the archaeologists located the submarine under three feet of mud near Sullivan's Island off the South Carolina coast, where she had lain for more than 130 years. Excavation of the craft continues as of this writing. The area has been declared a federal war grave where nine gallant men died. The Naval Historical Center in Washington, D.C., is also contributing its efforts to raise and preserve the *Hunley*.[42]

In 1872 another American submarine with a mysterious background made its appearance. American inventor Oliver Halstead first offered his creation to France, but the offer was declined. Some time later, an American general named William Dixie Hoxie built this submarine, dubbed *The Intelligent Whale*, a title derived from its general shape. This submarine was 30 feet long 8 1/2 feet in diameter and required a crew of six to operate her. She could travel at a speed of four knots and was lowered to the bottom by first dropping anchor weights, decreasing its buoyancy slightly, and then reeling the craft to the bottom. Divers could exit the craft through two doors in its bottom. On one of her initial trials, one of the doors was left ajar and, had the submarine not been supported by ropes, the crew would have been lost. The U.S. government purchased the submarine shortly after its trials and began its own experimentation with this craft. Several accounts of the experiments exist, and all read like horror stories. It is recorded that thirty-nine men drowned in the *Whale,* which eventually was abandoned and placed on exhibit, first in the Brooklyn Navy Yard and later at the U.S. Naval Museum in Washington, D.C., where she remains today.[43]

Another American inventor of submarines was a contemporary and competitor of Simon Lake. He was John Phillip Holland, the man on whom many historians bestow the title "Father of the Modern Submarine." Holland was an Irish immigrant who arrived in Boston in November of 1873 and turned his thoughts to submarines while recuperating from a fall that broke his leg. Teaching duties at the St. John's Parochial School in Patterson, New Jersey, forced him to ignore his plans until 1874, when his tutoring brought him into contact with Navy Secretary George M. Robeson. The secretary convinced him to submit his designs to the navy, and in February of 1875 he did so. The proposed submarine was a small, treadle-powered, one-man affair measuring 15 1/2 feet in length. The operator had to wear a diving suit because the cabin flooded during a dive. Compressed air was supplied from a tank within the submarine.

Naval officials were skeptical. Holland set about building his submarine and tested her in the Passaic River early in 1878. The actual craft was 14 1/2 feet long, 3 feet at the beam, and 2 1/2 feet high, weighing 2 1/2 tons. She was designated the *Holland I* and was square in cross section, tapering to a pointed bow. A small conning tower located amidships contained ports for keeping the craft on course.[44] The little submarine served to justify Holland's theories of underwater navigation.

Holland's Irish heritage assumed a major role in his submarine experimentation. The Fenian Brotherhood in the United States was attempting to generate financial and moral support for the Irish Rebellion against the British. Influential members of the clandestine organization became convinced that submarine harassment of the British Navy would further their cause. From its Skirmishing Fund, the Fenian Brotherhood provided Holland with $5,000 to construct the *Holland I.*[45] The craft was built at the Albany Iron Works. Holland installed a Brayton gasoline engine in his small craft, and on May 28, 1878, he launched the submarine. The *Holland I* went to the bottom. Fortunately, he had attached tow ropes to her, which

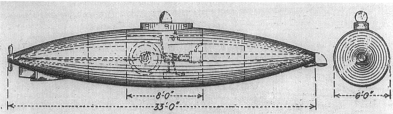

fig. 9. Model of John Holland's first submarine in the Patterson Museum, Patterson, New Jersey (*top;* courtesy Naval Historical Center) and a drawing of the craft by Simon Lake (*bottom;* courtesy J. B. Lippencott Company)

enabled him to retrieve the craft. A few days later, he attempted a second launch. This time the Brayton engine would not fire up, so Holland attached a line from the steam engine of an accompanying launch, ingeniously powering his gasoline engine with steam. He was off and running. After about a month of testing, Holland removed the engine and other usable components and scuttled his craft in the Passaic River near the Spruce Street Bridge. Fifty years later, the submarine was raised and given to the Patterson Museum.[46]

The "salt water enterprise," as members of the Fenians called Holland's efforts, had created a good deal of excitement within the organization. Holland began planning his second submarine. In May of 1879 he began work at the Delamater Iron Works on the craft that would become the *Fenian Ram*. This submarine required two years to complete at an estimated cost of sixty thousand dollars. Holland's creation lived up to all of his expectations and represents the most successful submarine of its time. She measured thirty-one feet in length with a six-foot beam. The thickness of her iron skin made her very strong and, along with her fifty tons of momentum, probably accounts for her being called a "ram." In a minor accident that would have seriously damaged another craft, Holland remarked, "We had a demonstration once by running into the end of our pile at six miles speed owing to my bad steering or forgetfulness of the tide. We split a twelve inch pile and lifted a horizontal tie having a load of four feet of stone ballast over it, and hurt nothing but the engineer's respect for good English."[47] Holland again employed a Brayton engine to power the *Ram* both above and below the surface, air for the engine when submerged being delivered from compressed air tanks while the exhaust was vented to the exterior. Her surface speed was nine miles per hour and slightly less below water. The *Ram* was a diving boat that porpoised through the water using its forward momentum to drive it underwater. This diving maneuver was controlled by diving planes in the rear of the craft, a design that became characteristic of all of Holland's submarines. She had a fixed center of gravity and a constant positive buoyancy. Holland needed a crew of three to operate the submarine; however, the third member was responsible only for its armament, a pneumatic gun that fired a one-hundred-pound projectile for a distance of fifty to sixty yards underwater, or three hundred yards over water.[48]

Holland calculated that he could remain in the craft for three days without surfacing and, on at least one occasion, was able to reach a depth of sixty feet, where he remained for an hour. He was pleased with the submarine's performance, remarking, "There is scarcely anything required of a good submarine boat that this one did not do well enough, or fairly well."[49] The *Ram* was a characteristic Holland submarine of the porpoising or diving type, which is exactly what Holland wanted.[50] He also constructed another submarine, a small, one-man version of the *Ram*, to test new ideas he had come up with. Meanwhile, members of the Fenians became dissatisfied with all the experimentation and lack of action against the British Navy. Late in November of 1883, members of the brotherhood towed the *Ram* and Holland's smaller submarine from New Jersey into New York Harbor on their way to New Haven, Connecticut. Off Manhattan, a storm blew in, flooding the smaller craft that was being towed behind the *Ram*. The lines holding the smaller submarine snapped, and she went to the bottom in 110 feet of water. The *Ram* survived the voyage, and members of the Fenians attempted to operate the sub in New Haven harbor until the harbormaster put an end to the antics, which were endangering shipping in the harbor. Holland's "good submarine boat" was hidden in a shed after her engine and other components were stripped from her. Still, her fate was better than that of most of the early submarines. In 1916 she was exhibited in Madison Square Garden to help raise money for the victims of the Irish Uprising of 1916. In 1927 the *Ram* found her final resting place at West Side Park, New Jersey, permanently exhibited a short distance from the Passaic River, where her sister sub, the *Holland I,* had made her debut.[51]

Holland found himself in the unenviable position of being a successful submarine inventor without the backing necessary to continue his work. Fortuitously, Holland was to meet Lieutenant William W. Kimble of the U.S. Navy, who had the interest and foresight to see the value of the inventor's works. Holland went to work as a draftsman for Ronald's Iron Works in New York, assisting George Brayton in improving his gasoline engine, but he retained a close association with the navy lieutenant. Kimble would ultimately become a major driving force behind the Navy Department's interest in submarines and the hiring of Holland as chief designer. The association between Holland and Kimble undoubtedly influenced the Navy's criteria to be met by submarine constructors and set the stage for the acceptance of Holland designs by the U.S. government.

While awaiting governmental action, Kimble introduced Holland to another inventor. Second Lieutenant Edmund L. Zalinski, U.S. Army, was an ordnance expert responsible for developing a number of artillery range-finding devices. He had also been on the faculty of the Massachusetts Institute of Technology (MIT), where he taught military science, and at the time he met Holland, he owned the Pneumatic Gun Company. The former MIT professor hired Holland and began making financial arrangements for the incorporation of the Nautilus Submarine Boat Company, which was to construct a submarine that would become known as the *Zalinski Boat.*[52]

Limited funding resulted in the cigar-shaped submarine being built as a steel frame covered with wood. Constructed in Brooklyn, New York, the craft was fifty feet in length with an amidships diameter of eight feet. As her building progressed, Holland became discouraged because inadequate funding prevented him from using the design he knew the submarine required. His displeasure with the craft further increased when, upon launch, it smashed into some pilings, tearing a gaping hole in her bottom. As with Holland's first submarine, the *Zalinski Boat* sank to the bottom. Raised and repaired, the sub did make several runs in the summer of 1886. In the winter of that year, the Nautilus Submarine Boat Company disbanded.[53]

It was during the intervening years that the U.S. government would develop a real interest in the construction of submarines initiated through the efforts of men like Lieutenant Kimble. The result would be the three navy submarine competitions discussed earlier. Holland would enter all three, while Simon Lake would enter only the last of the competitions. It is almost a certainty that, at this point in time, the two inventors held a good deal of respect for each other's efforts. But political and financial constraints being generated within the fledgling submarine industry would cause them to become staunch competitors. One wonders what would have occurred had Holland and Lake combined their inventive talents instead of dissipating so much of their energies on the problems associated with the competitive aspects of their companies.

By the end of the nineteenth century, the possibility that the submarine could become an adjunct to a naval fleet was being considered by a few naval authorities. Its development had followed a circuitous route. The trials and tribulations of American inventors as presented here were echoed in Europe, where numerous submarines were also built. The desire to use submarines for underwater warfare appears to have been ubiquitous and undoubtedly intrigued humankind long before recorded history. The improvements in underwater navigation in both the United States and Europe were built upon the successes and failures of preceding generations of inventors and, as indicated above, two major factors played significant roles in the construction and use of submarines, particularly military submarines. First was the need for propulsive technologies that would make the submarine a viable entity. For example, the development of reliable batteries as well as gasoline and diesel engines around the turn of the century provided the necessary elements of propulsion, replacing human muscle power and cumbersome steam engines. The second factor that influenced submarine development was the military and political acceptance of a clandestine weapon of war.[54] The change in attitude that occurred early in the twentieth century would set the stage for inventors such as Lake and Holland to advance submarine development to a point where it would play a major role during the First and Second World Wars. And the submarine's evolution continues into the present. Today, atomic submarines represent one of the most formidable weapons ever invented.

CHAPTER 3

The Thousand-Mile Journey

While my book, Twenty Thousand Leagues Under the Sea, is entirely a work of the imagination, my conviction is that all I said in it will come to pass. A thousand mile voyage in the Baltimore submarine boat is evidence of this.
—Jules Verne in a telegram to the New York Journal, 1898

The successful trials of the *Argonaut Junior* allowed Simon Lake to form the Lake Submarine Company in November of 1895. Although unable to finance the building of the military submarine depicted in his submission to the government, he generated sufficient private funding for the construction of a smaller craft, christened the *Argonaut*. She was built at the Columbian Iron Works, and in the future frequently would be referred to as the "Baltimore Submarine Boat." It was apparent from her design that Lake had returned to his original purpose for the submarine, that of underwater salvage. The Colombian Iron Works had also been chosen as the constructor of the U.S. government's first submarine, the Holland-designed *Plunger*. During the next two years, the side-by-side construction created an uneasiness between the two companies. However, it should be recalled that the Holland boat was being constructed for the U.S. Navy as a military craft, while the Lake submarine was being built for a dual purpose: first, for her employment as a commercial salvager, and, secondarily, to demonstrate the effectiveness of the Lake design. Still, a rivalry existed. The *Plunger* would be fraught with so many difficulties that it would never be accepted by the government and would finally be discarded. The Baltimore Submarine

Boat would make its mark on history and receive many accolades, including those of Jules Verne.[1]

There seems to be a nature-nurture relationship between an individual's heritable qualities and the mysterious forces that shape history, a sort of "being in the right place at the right time" phenomenon. A combination of the historical period and his family background set the stage for Simon Lake to become an inventor. The submarine, roller shades, a forerunner of the Caterpillar tractor, prefabricated housing, photolithographic processes, typesetting machines, shoe manufacture, and aquaculture all have one thing in common: the name Lake.

Simon Lake was born on September 4, 1866. This was a year after the capitulation of the Confederacy at Appomattax, a time when people were aware of and still discussing the Rebel *Davids*. Four years earlier, the battle of the *Monitor* and *Virginia* (formerly the *Merrimack*) had ushered in the age of the ironclad. The Whitehead torpedo, called the "devil's device," was designed during Lake's birth year and was destined to become the standard weaponry of the submarine. Halstead had completed the *Intelligent Whale*. The Fenian Brotherhood made its ill-fated attempt to invade Canada in 1866. John Holland was twenty-six years old, still residing in Ireland. He would emigrate to the United States some six years later, bringing with him his dreams for a submarine. Four years after Lake's birth, Jules Verne would pen his famous science fiction novel, *Twenty Thousand Leagues Under the Sea*. It was an interesting time, because recovery from the Civil War had sparked the inventive spirit in the United States, and this atmosphere would permeate Lake's childhood. Additionally, his unique family would imprint its mark upon his character.[2]

Lake was the only son of John Christopher and Miriam (Adams) Lake, of Pleasantville (formerly called Lakeville), New Jersey. According to his family's genealogy, his mother was a descendant of Jeremy Adams, who emigrated from England in 1632 to Cambridge, Massachusetts. That year Jeremy joined Thomas Hooker and became one of the founders and proprietors of Connecticut's capital city, Hartford. Jeremy was appointed Indian agent and keeper of the public inn, and he has gone down in history as one of the individuals responsible for hiding a charter that King George was attempting to force upon the Connecticut colonists. As the story goes, a group of prominent townsfolk were at Jeremy's home along with British representatives of the king. Windows were opened, causing the candles to be extinguished. The charter vanished, only to be found some time later in an old oak tree, subsequently known as the Charter Oak. His role in the so-called Charter Oak Affair resulted in his name being inscribed on the Founders' Monument at the old church burying ground in Hartford, Connecticut.

Lake's great-grandmother, Abigail Adams, was a direct descendant of Jeremy and became the wife of John Adams, second president of the United States. Her son, John Quincy Adams, would serve as secretary of state and compose the Monroe Doctrine. Later he would become the country's sixth president.[3] Simon Lake's maternal grandfather, Captain Elisha Adams, and his sons gained recognition for operating one of the country's first aquacultural endeavors. They would bring young oysters from the Chesapeake and Chincoteague Bays, seed them in Absecom Bay, and then harvest their crop once the shellfish matured. They also experimented with altering the salinity of the water surrounding seed oysters reared in holding tanks in their specially built oyster houses. The results were fat oysters with an improved flavor.[4]

Family tradition has it that the Lake line is of Welsh origin (Leake) and that family members migrated to England during the thirteenth century. A Sir Gerald Lake was knighted for his efforts in bringing India under British domination. In 1633 Simon Lake's paternal ancestor, John Lake, came to America, settling first in Massachusetts. He later moved to New Amsterdam, now New York. John was given a land grant on which he founded Gravesend, the area that was destined to become Brooklyn, New York. His son, William, became a successful whaler and broker in real estate and purchased a large tract of land in south New Jersey that was to become a hub for future generations of Lakes. The town was originally named Lakeville and later renamed Pleasantville. It has been suggested that the agriculturally impoverished nature of this region may have served as an impetus for the inventive skills so prevalent in the Lake family.[5]

During the colonial days prior to the American Revolution, family member Daniel Lake constructed large shallow basins along the shore of New Jersey for gathering salt. A later generation of Lakes, realizing that the tidal land was unsuited for agriculture, built a tourist's roadway across this marsh to the adjoining island. What was considered by the family to be a "worthless" piece of Lake land eventually became Atlantic City, New Jersey.[6]

The Lake household in Pleasantville must have been one large workshop in constant use. Lake himself once stated, "Tools run in our bloodstream and drawing boards and calipers are household necessities."[7] Lake's father, John Christopher Lake, invented and successfully marketed the roller window shade and was making a good living at it when Simon was born. His grandfather, after whom Simon was named, invented the first seed-planting machine as well as spreaders for fertilizers.[8]

Simon's mother died in 1869, when he was three years old. His father left him with his step-grandmother and his uncle while he went west to sell his roller shades. It would be Lake's uncle Jesse Lake who nurtured the boy's curiosity and gave him free reign of the workshop. Jessie worked with the construction crew building the roadway across the marsh to the island that would become Atlantic City. It was difficult work, particularly hard on the horses, which often sank up to their shoulders in mud. Horses were one of the main energy sources at this time, and they were often used to drive various farm machines by walking on the inside bottom track of the treadmills. Jessie's experimental work reversed this principle, having a horse walk on the upper track of the mill. His objective was to keep the horse above the surface being traversed, allowing the vehicle's lower track to move over the surface. It was similar (in principle) to a military tank. Unknowingly, he had formulated the basic idea of the Caterpillar tractor. Jessie next replaced the horse with a noisy steam engine when he grew unhappy with the slowness of his horse's progression across the marsh. "Lake's Hell Engine" was used to construct the turnpike to the Atlantic City seashore. Its name derived from the racket it made, but it did move thousands of tons of gravel. Some years later, when investigators employed by *Scientific American* were attempting to determine the origins of the Caterpillar tractor, they gave Jessie full credit for its design. He also invented automatic weighing machines and a whistling buoy. At his death in 1905, Jessie held sixty-five patents. But his most important contribution was the tutorage of his nephew.[9]

Simon Lake spent much of his youth in another of the small country towns in New Jersey, this one named Tom's River. All accounts indicate that he was a mischievous youth. His fiery red hair and freckled face frequently made him the target of the town's bullies. He always seemed to be in trouble, both in school and at home. One positive attribute seemed to be that he was an ardent reader and experimenter. He caused a good deal of excitement on the Tom's River one day when friends found his overturned canoe floating some distance from shore. When they righted it, Lake was found beneath it attempting to establish how long the entrapped air remained breathable.[10]

Lake completed his high school education and then attended the Clinton Liberal Institute at Fort Plain, New York, where he studied business principles. It did not take long for him to become bored with these studies. He returned home and went to work in his father's shop manufacturing roller shades and became his father's partner at the age of eighteen. His love of mechanics prompted him to enroll at the Franklin Institute in Philadelphia to study mechanical drawing. Dissatisfied with his factory work, Lake's mind turned to problems of the day requiring the inventive mind he possessed. He designed a mechanical movement that was applicable as a steering gear on many pieces of machinery, and he received his first patent (No. 363,473) for this new mechanism. He applied the mechanism to the high-wheeled bicycles of the time, making them much safer in steering a straight course. Next, he employed his device on oyster dredges and winders. This venture proved so successful that he moved to Baltimore to be closer to the oyster industry. It was here, in 1888, that he met Margaret Vogel, whom he married in 1890. Since the oyster boat machinery could be installed only during the evening, when the fleet was docked, Lake had the daylight hours to turn his attention to another bit of inventiveness. Baltimore also happened to be the headquarters of the canning industry. The capping of canned goods was done with a crude machine, requiring the tops to be soldered to the can by trained workers. These men were organized as the Cappers' Union of Baltimore. Generally, they worked in pairs and could cap fifteen thousand cans a day. Lake built a new machine that, during its first trial, was able to cap fifty thousand cans a day and only required two untrained men to keep the machine up and running. This situation did not sit well with the union, and its members threatened to call a strike at any factory using the Lake machine. Lake realized that the union would be helpless to stop the owners of the canning companies from installing these machines, as they did not require skilled labor to operate them. But now his lack of business acumen was to betray him and create a Catch-22 situation. He had one machine that would cap one- and two-pound cans, but the factory owners not only wanted more of these machines; they also wanted additional machines capable of capping three-pound cans. They refused to put up any additional money to back the building of the new machines. Unable to locate any backers because of the problems with the Cappers' Union, Lake relinquished his efforts and returned to his steering gear business.[11]

He did not have to wait long for a situation to develop that would require his inventive skills. One day in 1892, his wife, Margaret, excitedly brought to him the newspaper article describing the U.S. Navy's announcement of its third submarine competition. Reading the short announcement rekindled his childhood interest in submarines.[12] He entered the 1893 government competition and was rejected in favor of the designs of

John Holland. An interesting historical note here is that an Admiral Baird, who was at that time in charge of the Naval Board, told Lake that four of the five board members actually favored the Lake design, but because he had not submitted a bid, his plans were dismissed.[13] Holland, although elated with his success, responded with his subtle Irish humor. His comment obviously reflected his previous dealings with the various naval boards. Holland called upon the dictionary's definition of a "board" to verbalize his perception of these bureaucratic groups as "long, narrow and wooden."[14] Lake, most certainly, concurred, but his rejection set the stage for Lake to build his *Argonaut Junior.* The subsequent demonstration of the Lake prototype impressed a sufficient number of backers, permitting him to build the Baltimore submarine, the *Argonaut I.*

The keel for the *Argonaut I* was laid in 1895 at the Colombian Iron Works. Her thirty-six-foot length was dwarfed by the government's eighty-five-foot *Plunger,* which was being built alongside her by the Holland company. Although Lake and Holland were later to see each other on a regular basis, there appears to have been no personal contact between them at this time. "The rivalry between the two companies was based not merely on business and professional[ism] but also on intensely personal considerations. The Holland people were able to say that the Navy Department had given them the contract, but on the other hand several of the practical shipbuilders in the company which was building the *Plunger* had taken stock in the Lake enterprise."[15]

The cast-iron hull of the *Argonaut* took the shape of an elongated egg turned on its side. Two large steel wheels, seven feet in diameter, were located forward, with a small steering wheel aft. The craft measured thirty-six feet, nine inches in length and nine feet in diameter. She would displace fifty-nine tons. Power both above and below the water's surface was delivered from a thirty-horsepower White and Middleton gasoline engine. Initially, air was delivered to the engine and exhaust gases were removed through a pair of canvas hoses that floated above the craft. These were later replaced by two fifty-foot-long masts that worked more efficiently. The length of these pipes effectively determined the normal operating depth of the submarine (less than fifty feet). Deeper dives of shorter duration were possible because the pipes were valved like modern snorkles for deeper submergence. Lake believed that this fifty-foot depth was adequate for the type of salvaging work the *Argonaut* was designed for. In the bow was Lake's characteristic diver's chamber and a powerful searchlight. Air compressors, both hand operated and motor driven, were used for ballast control and providing air for breathing when the craft remained under-

fig. 10 The *Argonaut I* during her construction. From Simon Lake, *The Argonaut: Her Evolution and History, What She Was Built For and What She Has Accomplished* (Altantic Highlands, N.J.: Lake Submarine Company, 1899)

water for extended periods. The *Argonaut* did not possess the hydroplanes Lake used in subsequent submarines for even-keel diving.[16] He used two methods to submerge the *Argonaut:* he could sink to the bottom simply by flooding her ballast tanks, or he could use two anchor weights, fore and aft and each weighing one thousand pounds, which could be lowered to the sea bottom. After adjusting the water ballast, the submarine could be reeled to the bottom. Further adjustments in the ballast permitted the wheels to bite into the substratum so that the craft could begin to crawl over the bottom. The crew of five as well as the engine received fresh air from the surface through the intake mast. The submarine could dive below her normal fifty-foot depth for up to twenty-four hours because the mast was fitted with a valve that closed when the craft reached depths greater than fifty feet. Under conditions of complete submergence, air was supplied from two steel cylinders containing compressed air. This reserve permitted the crew to remain underwater for twenty-four hours before having to surface.

Lake had patented the *Argonaut* on April 5, 1893 (U.S. Patent No.

469,109), and two years later he patented a salvaging device called the submarine locomotive and wrecking cars (No. 570,043), to be used in conjunction with the *Argonaut.* These patents were turned over to his company, the Lake Submarine Company, on February 8, 1896.[17] He was now ready to begin trials with the *Argonaut* and, once those tests were completed, begin salvaging cargoes from a number of wrecks in the Chesapeake Bay area. During these trials he received a visit from Col. Charles Hasker of Richmond, Virginia. Col. Hasker was one of two survivors of the Confederate *Hunley,* and, although still leery of submarines, he was pleased to see the advancements that had been made since the Civil War. He was kind enough to provide Lake with a thorough description of the *Hunley* that was sufficient for Lake to commission the now famous painting presented in most historical treatments of the submarine.[18]

As the *Argonaut* was nearing completion, the country went to war with Spain. Seeing this as an opportunity to interest the government in his submarine, Lake contacted then Secretary of the Navy Theodore Roosevelt, suggesting possible deployment of his craft. The secretary was particularly interested in the diving chamber from which divers could exit and clear harbors of minefields. Roosevelt told Lake that a board would be appointed to study the applicability of his submarine to such an endeavor. In the interim, however, Roosevelt resigned from the navy and joined the army to lead his Rough Riders during the Spanish-American War. The naval board was never called. Discouraged, Lake took the *Argonaut* to Hampton Roads and tried to interest army officials at Fort Monroe in her. The army, at this time, was responsible for guarding the entrance to Chesapeake Bay. When these discussions failed, Lake decided to locate and map the army's minefields in the bay from his submarine. He delivered his map showing the location of the mines and their cables was told in no uncertain terms that, if he were ever to enter the bay again, he would be arrested and imprisoned. Two navy officers did, unofficially, visit the *Argonaut.* They requested permission from the navy to make a dive in the submarine but were denied for two reasons. One was that officers were too few in number to risk their lives on a submarine. And second, the navy already had its own submarine (the ill-fated *Plunger*) and would not consider looking at a second craft until the capabilities of the first were adequately demonstrated.[19]

Lake had the opportunity to try out one of his many "firsts" for a submarine while testing the *Argonaut* in the Patapsco River near Baltimore. He installed a telephone in his sub and became the first individual to make an underwater telephone call. In fact, two calls were made. One

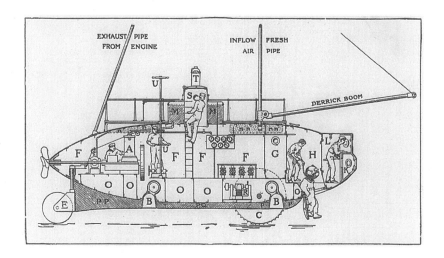

fig. 11. Internal aspects of the *Argonaut I* and an artist's rendering of the submarine salvaging a wreck. From Lake Submarine Company, *Submarine Engineering* (Bridgeport, Conn.: Lake Submarine Company, 1906)

was to William T. Malster, mayor of Baltimore, and a second to the president of the Chesapeake and Potomac Telephone Company in Washington, D.C.[20]

In July of 1898, the *Argonaut* went five miles out into the Atlantic Ocean off Cape Henry. She was escorted by the tug *Annie,* out of Norfolk, Virginia, during this trial. A severe squall came up while the sub was below the surface. When the *Argonaut* returned to the surface, the tug was rolling her rails under. Lake and his crew had been totally unaware of the storm while below the surface, but when they surfaced the little submarine was buffeted by the storm. Lake decided to return to the bottom to wait it out. The storm subsided, and during the return voyage, Lake expressed his pleasure with the manner in which his submarine had weathered such a heavy sea. He began planning a longer voyage. To enhance the *Argonaut's* performance in the open ocean, he decided that it would be necessary to lengthen her and add a more shiplike superstructure after her preliminary tests.

Once the initial trials and testing of the *Argonaut* had been completed, Lake felt it was time for a real test of her seaworthiness. He set out from Norfolk, Virginia, and headed his craft into the open ocean. The voyage would last two months as he worked his way up the Atlantic coastline, stopping at various locations to renew his fuel and food stores and to make repairs. During the trip the *Argonaut* would travel unescorted on the surface. She would regularly dive to test her underwater capabilities and investigate a number of wrecks that that had been located. When the seas became too heavy for surface navigation, the *Argonaut* would simply drop below the surface and cruise along out of harm's way. Lake was proud of his little submarine. A log entry from July 28, 1898, provides insight into how smoothly things were going for the crew:

> Submerged at 8:20 A.M. in about thirty feet of water. Temperature in the living compartment, eighty-three degrees Fahrenheit. Compass bearing west-north-west, one-quarter-west. Quite a lively sea running on the surface, also strong current. At 10:45 A.M. shut down engine; temperature eighty-eight degrees Fahrenheit.
>
> After engine was shut down, we could hear the wind blowing past our pipes extending above the surface; we could also tell by the sound when any steamers were in the vicinity. We first allowed the boat to settle gradually to the bottom, with the tide running ebb; after a time the tide changed, and she would

work slightly sideways; we admitted about 400 pounds of water additional, but she would move occasionally, so that a pendulum nine inches long would sway one-eighth of an inch (thwartship). At 12 o'clock (noon) temperature was eighty-seven degrees Fahrenheit. There were no signs of carbonic acid gas at 2:45, although the engine had been closed down for three hours and no fresh air had been admitted during the time. Could hear the whistle of boats on the surface, and also their propellers when running close to the boat. At 3:30 the temperature had dropped to eighty-five degrees. At 3:45 found a little sign of carbonic acid gas, very slight, however, as a candle would burn fairly bright in the pits. Though we could detect a smell of gasoline by comparing the fresh air which came down the pipe (when the hand blower was turned). Storage lamps were burning during the five hours of submergence, while engine was not running.

At 3:50 engine was again started, and went off nicely. Went into diving compartment and opened door; came out through air-lock and left pressure there; found the wheels had buried about ten inches or one foot, as the bottom had several inches of mud. We had 500 pounds of air in the tanks, and it ran the pressure down to 250 pounds to open the door in about thirty feet.

The temperature fell in the diving compartment to eighty-two degrees after the compressed air was let in.

Cooked clam fritters and coffee for supper. The spirits of the crew appeared to improve the longer we remained below; the time was spent in catching clams, singing, trying to waltz, playing cards, and writing letters to wives and sweethearts.[21]

The little craft continued its trek up the coast, finally docking at Sandy Hook, New Jersey, in November of 1898. She had weathered the storms of October and November, during which, according to Lake, more than two hundred vessels were lost. This exaggerated statement concerning vessel loss appears in a number of Lake's writings, but it may be accurate if one counts rowboats, sailboats, and so forth. Regardless, the *Argonaut* had completed a voyage of over one thousand miles, much of it in the open ocean without escort vessels. Waiting for Lake on shore was the congratulatory telegram from his spiritual mentor, Jules Verne. The thousand-mile voyage of the *Argonaut* had covered approximately 350 leagues.

fig. 12. The *New Argonaut* after modifications to make her more seaworthy. She was rechristened the *Argonaut II*. From Lake Torpedo Boat Company, *The Development of the Lake Type Submarine* (Bridgeport, Conn.: Lake Torpedo Boat Company, 1906)

During the winter of 1898–99, Lake began to modify the *Argonaut*. His open ocean voyage indicated that the submarine could be made even more seaworthy if she were lengthened and provided with more deck space and a greater fuel capacity. The lengthening would also make it more comfortable for the crew by providing larger living quarters. Lake felt that the modifications would give the *Argonaut* an operating range of three thousand miles and space for a crew of eight. The craft was brought to J. N. Robbins Dry Dock Company in Brooklyn, New York, where she was cut in half and lengthened to fifty-six feet. The *New Argonaut*, or *Argonaut II*, as she was now called, was taken to Bridgeport, Connecticut, where Lake had decided to set up his company's headquarters.[22]

While Lake busied himself with his new company, he would, on occasion, take groups of people on underwater excursions. One of these trips was particularly memorable. He had invited twenty-two people for what was to be a short jaunt in Bridgeport Harbor. The group included Hugh Sterling, mayor of Bridgeport, J. C. Spiers, superintendent of the Locomobile Company, G. E. Betts, manager of the New England Telephone Company, and nineteen other guests representing other companies and political offices important to the financial well-being of Bridgeport. The group was a lively one, and its members were fascinated with being on the bottom of the harbor. One member, John Fisher, was a noted singer and recording artist for the local phonograph company, and he began entertaining the other members of the group with his version of "Down Went

McGinty." The crew prepared and dished out helpings of clam chowder. Small groups entered the diving chamber to view the harbor's bottom. No one was keeping track of the time—except the people on shore. As the hours went by, fear began to develop in the onlookers. A tug was sent out and was able to locate the *Argonaut*'s mast projecting above the water's surface. The captain of the tug rapped several times on the pipe, but there was no answer. Between the singing and the conversations going on below, no one heard the rapping. The tug headed back to the dock with the sad report that all aboard the sub had drowned. A call was placed to the Merritt and Chapman Wrecking Company of New York to send a wrecking barge to the scene. The news spread like a grass fire that the mayor of Bridgeport and his associates had been lost in a submarine accident. However, at four o'clock that afternoon, a small craft with flags flying from its fifty-foot mast was seen entering the harbor. There was both elation and anger at the sight of the *Argonaut*.[23]

CHAPTER 4

Salvaging the Riches of the Sea

> The sinking of ships goes back to the days when navigation began and, according to statistics, the value of the entire commerce of the world at any one time is lost every twenty-five years.
>
> —*Simon Lake*

There is a tradition at Lloyds of London in which, upon the news that one of the company's insured vessels has sunk, the bell from the old frigate *La Lutine* is rung. Hardly a day passes that the old bell is not sounded. Nautical maps that chart the locations of sunken vessels give the appearance of well-used dartboards. In many instances, the depth at which these ships sank is too great for them to be reached even with our most modern deep-diving equipment. A large number, however, lie strewn in the shallower coastal waters, awaiting the adventurous soul seeking his or her fortune. With the proper equipment, the wrecking business can be a profitable, though dangerous and costly one.[1]

Like many young men, Simon Lake was fascinated with the thought of sunken treasure. Unlike most, he set out to realize his dreams. The *Argonaut* had been lengthened and a new superstructure added to enhance her seaworthiness. Now designated the *Argonaut II,* she was operating better than her inventor's expectations. Lake began charting the wrecks in Long Island Sound from his headquarters in Bridgeport, Connecticut. He had also built a surface ship he called his "wreck-finding vessel." Unfortunately, the company's secrets surrounding this craft and the devices it was equipped with have remained just that. The methods Lake employed to locate sunken cargoes with this vessel have not been revealed. A description of the submarine's effectiveness reads:

> In this locality the bottom was rocky and the current swift—about three knots an hour—but not withstanding these difficulties, a territory of about 50 square miles was thoroughly covered in two weeks' time. Where the bottom is sandy or free of rocks and boulders, the search can be carried on at a rate of about 30 square miles a day. The means employed call for the construction of special wreck-finding boats equipped with special machinery and electrical appliances of Mr. Lake's invention . . ., but as the method of its employment and the apparatus are important trade secrets the Company naturally withholds further details for obvious reasons.[2]

Within a short time of using the wreck finder, Lake was able to locate sixteen sunken vessels. In only two of these cases were the locations even approximately known. Fourteen of the wrecks were unrecorded, and he was never able to establish their identities.[3] One wreck typified Lake's proficiency at locating and salvaging sunken vessels. An old sea captain had told him of a ship owned by the Thames Towboat Company that had been consigned to the Oldroyd Copper Company out of Brooklyn, New York. She had gone down in a violent storm during 1892 carrying a load of copper oar and copper matte. Immediately, the owners sent out a tug to locate her but failed. A superintendent of the company knowledgeable of the cargo's value fitted out an expedition and began searching for her. After two years, the search was called off. When Lake went searching in 1897, it took him only two days to find her off Hammonasset Point. The cargo was salvaged and sold to its original owners at a handsome profit for the Lake Submarine Company, starting Simon Lake on the road to his multimillionaire status.[4]

Numerous coal-laden barges had sunk in Long Island Sound. Lake designed and built an ingenious device for salvaging the coal. He called this device his submarine locomotive or wrecking car. It was cylindrical in shape and was towed behind the *Argonaut*. At the wreck sight, the unit was filled with water and sunk. Once it was on the bottom, a diver from the *Argonaut* opened the top, and coal was pumped in by means of a powerful suction pump. The wrecking car was closed, and the water it

fig. 13. Nautical maps that Lake used to illustrate the abundance of wrecks in the offshore waters of the United States and Europe. From Lake Submarine Company, *Submarine Engineering* (Bridgeport, Conn.: Lake Submarine Company, 1906)

contained was pumped out, allowing it to rise to the surface in much the same way as a submarine surfaces. This device permitted the recovery of three tons of coal an hour. Smaller grades of coal (called nut coal) were even easier to handle. Using a six-inch pump, Lake could transfer fifteen tons of nut coal in ninety minutes. He calculated that it cost him fifty cents a ton to retrieve the coal, but it sold for several dollars a ton at the dock. Coal is not damaged by submersion in water. In fact, saltwater submergence appears to make the coal burn hotter and more completely, lending credence to housewives' stoking early-morning coal stoves by sprinkling a little table salt into them.[5]

Other types of cargoes were more challenging. Cast iron rusts and becomes welded in a large mass in seawater. To salvage it, the divers had to cut the mass into smaller bundles before it was brought to the surface. Lake even salvaged cargoes of tanned hides that had been under water for

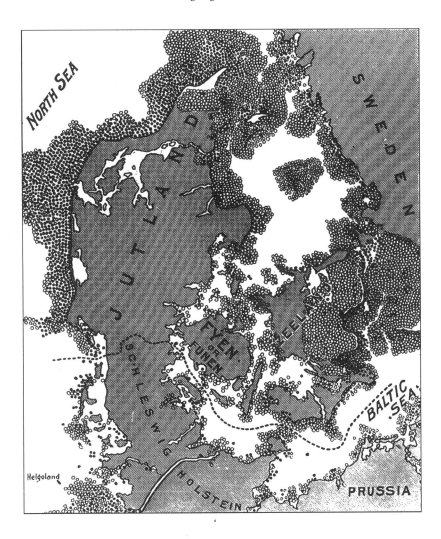

a number of years. Barrels of flour that remained watertight were brought up and found to be in salable condition. But there were times when, after locating a wreck and getting lines attached to it, the divers would find it loaded with stones or oyster shells. These were left undisturbed.[6]

Working around sunken wrecks could be dangerous, especially when bottom currents were running strong enough to shift the *Argonaut*'s position. The divers, exiting through the hatch, often worked in relays. This introduced a problem: a new relay of divers could overlook a shift in the position of the submarine caused by strong currents. Such an event occurred once while Lake was working on a wreck. The work for the day had been completed, and when he started to blow the ballast tanks, the

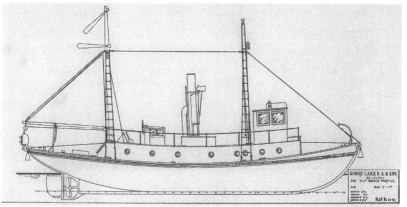

fig. 14. Lake's cargo-recovering device (*top*) and his wreck-finding vessel (*bottom*). From Lake Submarine Company, *Submarine Engineering* (Bridgeport, Conn.: Lake Submarine Company, 1906)

Argonaut would not budge. Lake sent his diver out to investigate. The current had pushed the submarine under an overhang created by the wreck, and the tiny craft could not break free. Further, there was so much debris around the area that the diver feared they would snap off the propeller if they tried to back out. Lake must have been one very cool-headed individual, because his solution to the problem was to sit there until the tide changed and, as Lake said, "not tell each other ghost stories."[7] The plan worked, and the uneasy submariners made their way to the surface as soon as the *Argonaut's* nose had been freed.

Lake's salvaging operations were receiving a good deal of attention from the press, and the reputation he developed as a finder of lost ships was to stay with him for the rest of his life. For example, after World War I he began contemplating the salvaging of the *Lusitania*. One day he received a letter from a woman who had been a passenger on the ill-fated ship. It read:

> Dear Mr. Lake,
>
> I see by the newspapers that you are about to undertake the salvaging of the *Lusitania*'s cargo. If this is the truth, I wish to ask you to do me a very great favor. Do you mind recovering my $100,000 diamond necklace? I value it not only for its intrinsic value, but because my husband gave it to me. Finding it will be a simple matter. It is under my pillow in my bed in Stateroom 357 Deck B.[8]

Lake's inventive mind continued to generate applications for the technology he was developing. He was a man unable to rest on his laurels, constantly pushing the envelope of invention. His granddaughter, Wyn Oldroyd, once commented, "He was never interested in the money he made. The few million he did make he just invested in another project. His love was in the inventing."[9] An example of this love for inventing was witnessed as he cruised the bottom of Long Island Sound. He was amazed at the acres of oysters and the ease with which he could collect them from the *Argonaut*'s diving chamber. What appeared shortly thereafter on his drawing board was a design for a submarine to be used by oystermen for the efficient harvest of vast quantities of shellfish. It could be accomplished in comfort below the water's surface from his submarine. This design never reached fruition.

Lake appeared to have another passion, that of starting new companies (see Appendix B). In 1899 he founded the Submarine Exploration and Recovery Company in Bridgeport, Connecticut, apparently to expand his base of operations and generate more capital for his research. By 1901 he had salvaged thirty wrecks and reaped the fortunes of his underwater odyssey. He purchased a white-pillared mansion that still stands on Broad Street across from the green in Milford, Connecticut. Today this beautiful mansion is a funeral home. Still present in the hallway is an antique grandfather clock that Lake purchased in Germany. It is said that this timepiece once belonged to Frederick the Great, and it still ticks away the time as it did in the 1740s. The inventor and salvager moved into his new home with his family, which now included his wife Margaret, their daughters Margaret and Miriam, and their son, Thomas Alva Edison Lake, named after the inventor whom Lake held in highest esteem. It was a

happy time for Lake and his family. He became one of the founders of
the Blackrock Country Club in Fairfield, Connecticut. His rationale for
establishing this club reflects the personality of the man. The internal iner-
tia that drove this inventor caused him to become involved in many projects that required a great deal of traveling. A man of temperance, Lake
was always disappointed with the bawdy behavior he witnessed in hotels
where he resided during his many business trips. The club he helped
found provided a respectable alternative to the hotels of the day as no
drinking or smoking were allowed and, of course, no women were permitted in rooms.

It was also during this period that Lake conceived the idea of traveling
under the North Pole by submarine. He presented this idea during a talk
given at Johns Hopkins University, and it generated such interest that
there was talk of Joseph Pulitzer financing the expedition. However, it
would be thirty years before Lake would implement this particular idea.[10]

The fertile mind of Simon Lake continued to develop numerous
mechanisms for the salvaging of the ocean's riches. His company's adver-
tisements from these early years indicate that, in addition to his successful
wrecking operation, he was now expanding into other aspects of undersea
work. He designed equipment for the construction of breakwaters, light-
houses, piers, and abutments. The equipment could also be employed for
the deepening and improvement of harbors and waterways. He developed
a new system for tunnel construction that was particularly applicable to
underwater work. The fascination he had witnessed in passengers he had
taken below the surface led him to design a craft for pleasure as well as
scientific descents into the deep. He proposed methods for the retrieval of
gold, sponges, and pearls from the ocean floor. But of all his designs, the
one that would be unique to Lake would be his "salvage tube."[11]

Always concerned with safety, especially that of his divers, Lake sought
a way to lessen the dangers of working at the high pressures that divers
were subjected to when underwater. In the days before the self-contained
breathing apparatus (SCUBA), divers used helmets fitted with a long air
hose, the so-called hard-hat rig. For every foot that a diver descends underwater, there is an increase of pressure of 0.43 pounds on each square
inch of the diver's body. At sea level the body experiences an air pressure
of 14.7 pounds per square inch. At a depth of, say, 130 feet, the diver experiences approximately four times the normal air pressure, or about 60
pounds per square inch of body surface. This increased pressure, de-
pending on how long the diver remains at a particular depth, causes more

air to dissolve into the blood, in much the same way that carbon dioxide is forced into water for the purpose of carbonating it. If the return to the surface by a diver is too fast, the gases bubble out of his bloodstream like the bubbles of gas in a bottle of soda when the top is removed. The presence of air bubbles, or emboli, in the bloodstream can result in caisson disease, or what divers call "the bends." The air bubbles lodge in the body's blood vessels, causing severe pain and often death. To prevent this situation from occurring, divers must ascend at a prescribed rate, permitting the air to slowly diffuse from their bloodstream, a process that can require a good deal of time and limit the effective working time of a diver on the bottom. This is but one of the hazards that all divers face. The hard-hat diver is also subjected to the danger of entangling the hoses that provide him with air.

Lake sought a method that would provide a greater margin of safety for his divers and allow them to spend additional time on the bottom. He returned to his idea of the diver's hatch in his submarine and simply placed it, along with its air lock, at the end of a long tube. The "salvage tube," as he referred to it, was attached at one end to a flexible cowling located on the mother ship while the other end was lowered to the wreck site. The distal end of the tube housed the air lock and the diver's chamber with its hatch that permitted access to the sea bottom. The air in the tube remained at normal sea level pressure, allowing the diver to descend stairs to the air lock. Once inside the lock, the pressure was raised to that inside the diver's chamber. This pressure was determined by the working depth and was just sufficient to prevent water from entering. At this point, the diver would don his helmet and waterproof suit and exit out onto the seabed. Upon completing his work, he would reenter the diver's chamber, to be replaced by a second diver, and then enter the air lock for slow decompression. In this way, the diving gear was immediately available to the second diver. The lengths of hose required were significantly less for a diver umbilicaled to the submarine than would be needed if he were to dive from the surface. Further, the decompressing diver did not tie up crew members at the surface, ensuring that he was hauled in according to rates specified in the decompression tables.[12]

The idea for the tube was to lie dormant until Lake ceased building submarines for the government in the early 1920s, at which time Lake would again return to salvaging. He would build a tube in the United States and another in England. Although he would consider using the latter device to salvage the *Lusitania,* the depth of the wreck made it infea-

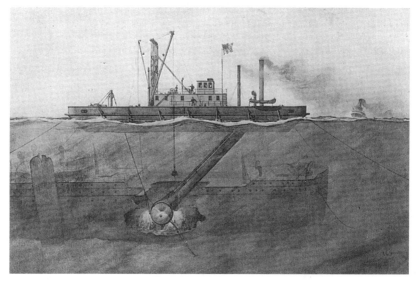

fig. 15. A drawing of Lake's salvage tube. From Lake Submarine Company, *Submarine Engineering* (Bridgeport, Conn.: Lake Submarine Company, 1906)

---

sible. The English tube was never used. Almost two decades later, however, he would build another tube and employ it in the last treasure hunt of his life.

The Spanish-American War seemed to have sparked a desire in Simon Lake to make a second attempt at interesting the U.S. government in his submarine designs, particularly in light of his success with the *Argonaut* and John Holland's failure with the *Plunger*. This would be the start of Lake's initiation into the world of politics and industrial espionage.

Holland's *Plunger* was finally launched in August of 1897, about the same time as the *Argonaut I*. On October 13, a valve was inadvertently left open and the *Plunger* went to the bottom at dockside. Frank Cable, who had gone to work for Holland and would later command the navy's first submarine during her trials, was an ingenious individual. The sub had remained submerged for eighteen hours and completely filled with water. Once she was raised to the surface, it was urgent that the electrical wiring be dried, or the submarine would need complete rewiring. When heaters failed to rid the wiring of the water, Cable gambled and reversed the electrical current in the system to generate enough heat to dry the wiring. But even with ingenious efforts like this, the *Plunger* was doomed to failure. She never got beyond the dock at the Colombian Iron Works except for her initial disposal in New Suffolk, Long Island. She was finally towed to the submarine base at New London, Connecticut, where she was sunk and used for diver training. The reason for its failure lay with the navy. Illness during the later stages of the *Plunger's* construction forced Holland to turn over its supervision to inexperienced naval officers who apparently attempted to incorporate any and all suggestions made by naval personnel. As Holland put it, the submarine had been "over-engineered." Realizing that the boat was a failure, Holland went to work on the smaller *Holland,* ultimately the U.S. Navy's first submarine.[13] But this is only the beginning of the story.

Gloating and yet sympathizing with Holland's problems with his steam-driven monster, Lake wrote to President McKinley the following letter:

The Lake Submarine Company
New York Office:
Bowling Green Building, 11 Broadway

Hon. Wm. McKinley
President of the United States

Dear Sir:

I understand there is a proposition before Congress to build additional submarine torpedo boats. As the inventor of a type of submarine boat that is well adapted to the needs of the government as submarine torpedo boats for either harbor or coast defense or for purposes of blockading or destroying fleets in foreign waters or for destroying mines or cutting cables, I think it would be to the great advantage of the government if the merits of my type of vessel were investigated. In 1893, I submitted plans to the then Secretary of the Navy under an advertisement requesting inventors to submit plans—these plans were returned with a letter from the Secretary stating that as they were not in accordance with the regulations they could not be considered—this not withstanding the fact that the circular distinctly stated if the plans submitted were informal they would be considered. Fortunately my type of vessel was as well adapted for commercial purposes as for war. Since that time I have devoted my attention largely to that branch of the business. The "Argonaut" is well known as the first entirely successful submarine boat ever built. Her efficiency was shown in 1897. I have sev-

fig. 16. John Holland emerging from the conning tower of the *Holland* (*top*); right figure shows the launch of the *Holland,* the Navy's first submarine, at Elizabethport, New Jersey, 1897. Courtesy Naval Historical Center

eral times tried to interest the government in the invention, but have fail probably through my inexperience in that line.

Several foreign governments have, however, shown great interest in her and have requested me through their representatives in Washington to submit plans. This I have not done as there are several features about my method of operating the submarine that I have discovered in my many years [of] study and experiment that I have not disclosed to anyone and which I consider of sufficient importance for our government to keep a secret (if they so wish).

I send under another cover a pamphlet on the "Argonaut" which only relates to the commercial advantages of vessels of the type and would be glad to submit to the proper authorities my plans for submarine torpedo vessels.

I do not know just the proper procedure to get the merits of my type of vessel investigated, but as I have failed to receive recognition here-to-fore, I take this liberty of writing you on the subject.

I am also writing the Secretary of the Navy and others, and

believe if an investigation is made where I can submit plans and have a hearing, I can convince anyone of the great value of this type of vessel to our government.

Yours Very Respectfully,
Simon Lake[14]

He received no reply from McKinley.

Sometime in 1900, Lake made one of the boldest decisions of his life. He founded the Lake Torpedo Boat Company in Bridgeport, Connecticut, where he planned to build military submarines. This was a marked deviation from his original intention for submarines. However, Simon Lake was not only a successful inventor and salvager; he was also a staunch American patriot. Nationalism, particularly as predicated by men like Theodore Roosevelt, was a driving force in the United States at the time, and Lake was affected by it. One can almost read this in Lake's portrait (frontispiece), in which he bears a striking resemblance to Roosevelt. The United States was on its way to becoming a world power, and its navy had finally recognized the value of submarines. Congress had authorized another appropriation for submarine construction, exemplifying the navy's change of heart toward these underwater craft. Lake had demonstrated a successful craft while the Holland Torpedo Boat Company was still struggling to get the navy's first boat in the water. Yet he could not generate government interest in his accomplishments. The Lake Torpedo Boat Company was a gamble, but he intuitively knew he could build the kind of submarines the country needed. Lake began constructing the *Protector,* the submarine that he would consider his most outstanding achievement.[15]

Meanwhile, the Holland Torpedo Boat Company faced difficulties of their own. By the summer of 1896, Holland had recognized the inadequacies of the *Plunger,* and by September he had completed his design for the *Holland.* Now began Holland's indoctrination into big business. Holland's company had been awarded the $200,000 government contract for the *Plunger.* But this sub was dead in the water, and its funding could not be applied to Holland's new design. At that point, there appeared a man of obvious foresight and rugged business acumen. Isaac Rice owned an electrical battery company as well as the Electric Launch Company. He had built electric launches for the families of such notables as Cornelius Vanderbilt, John Jacob Astor, Nathan Meyer Rothschild, and Grand Duke Alexander of Russia. So impressed was Rice with Holland's design and his past experiences with submarine construction that he bought the Holland Torpedo Boat Company, making it a subsidiary of his newly formed conglomerate, the Electric Boat Company. This company would ultimately become a subsidiary of General Dynamics and later build many of the atomic submarines. Realizing that he could profit from the naval contract held by Holland's company, Rice used it as a wedge to generate additional stock options to fund the building of the *Holland*. He was successful in obtaining the necessary funding, receiving a major contribution of twenty-five thousand dollars from a Mrs. Isaac Lawrence of New York.[16]

In late 1896, Holland began work on the *Holland* in the Crescent Shipyards at Elizabeth, New Jersey. The submarine was fifty-three feet, ten inches in length, with a ten-foot, three-inch beam. The height from bottom to superstructure deck was ten feet, seven inches, and the boat had a submerged displacement of 74.3 tons. A forty-five-horsepower, four-cycle Otto gasoline engine was used for surface running. The same engine was used to power the electric motor on the surface when it was used as a generator to recharge the batteries. Below the surface, the sub was powered by a single electric motor capable of generating fifty horsepower, providing a speed of eight knots. The *Holland*'s armament consisted of one lower deck tube in the bow for firing a Whitehead torpedo and a deck gun for the discharge of high explosive shells. The *Holland* was designed as a diving submarine, which maintained a positive buoyancy and used the propulsion of the motor to drive her under the surface.[17] Through a number of devices and the aft location of the rudder and diving planes, Holland was able to overcome many of the difficulties encountered by other inventors with the diving-type submarine.[18]

On the April 20, 1898, the *Holland* was observed by the Navy Board of Inspection, at which time two dives were made (one of thirty-eight minutes, the other lasting fifty-eight minutes). A dummy torpedo and aerial projectile were fired. The sub was offered to the navy at this point but was rejected by the board despite an earlier recommendation by Assistant Secretary of the Navy Theodore Roosevelt, who had written:

THEODORE ROOSEVELT
ASST. SECRETARY
NAVY DEPARTMENT
Washington,
April 10, 1898

My Dear Mr. Secretary:

I think that the Holland submarine boat should be purchased. Evidently she has in her great possibilities for harbor defense. Sometimes she doesn't work perfectly, but often she does, and I don't think that in the present emergency we can afford to let her slip. I recommend that you authorize me to enter into negotiations for her, or that you authorize the Bureau of Construction to do so, which would be just as well.

Very sincerely yours,
T. Roosevelt[19]

The "present emergency" Roosevelt was referring to was the saber rattling going on between the United States and Spain over the repressive subjugation of Cuban inhabitants. The day after the Naval Board inspected the *Holland,* the Spanish-American War erupted. It should be remembered that about that time Simon Lake had completed his one-thousand-mile voyage and had also mapped the minefields in the waters around Fort Monroe. Yet the government would still not recognize these accomplishments. Further, in December of 1899, Frank Cable sailed the *Holland* to Washington for purposes of exhibition. Newspaper reporters lauded the five-hundred-mile journey as a first for a submarine, ignorant of Lake's thousand-mile voyage, much of it in the open ocean, not the inland waterway traveled by the *Holland.*

While the *Holland* was on exhibition in Washington, Clara Barton, founder of the Red Cross, made a dive in the submarine. Upon exiting the sub, she castigated men like Holland and Lake, saying that she was surprised that any American would be guilty of inventing such a deadly instrument of war.[20]

The various naval authorities investigating the *Holland* were hesitant to acknowledge final acceptance of this submarine to the secretary of the navy. Most were also resistant to considering another design while their first submarine was still under construction. This reluctance placed both fledgling submarine companies in a precarious situation. However, while the U.S. government mulled over its predicament, other governments were making overtures to both the Electric Boat Company and the Lake Torpedo Boat Company.

CHAPTER 5

The Plunger Affair

In politics, nothing happens by accident. If it happens, you can bet it was planned that way.
—Franklin D. Roosevelt

According to some psychologists, proficiency in chess requires an aptitude in four aspects of intelligence: memory, visualization, organization, and imagination. It is a contest between two opponents with considerable ego involvement and represents a play-substitute for the art of war.[1] One can readily understand why chess is often taught at military colleges and the frequent involvement of industrialists with the game.

So it was with Isaac Rice, the man who was responsible for absorbing the Holland Torpedo Boat Company into the larger conglomerate known as the Electric Boat Company. Rice would become known not only for his shrewd operation of this company, but also for the Rice Gambit in chess. Of his many accomplishments, two mark his successes: his foresight for the promotion of electrical inventions, which led to his involvement with submarines, and his practice of law, which provided inside information on the functioning of large corporations. Life was, indeed, his chess game. For example, during the money panic of 1907, he lost his holding in all of the companies in which he had invested, save for his stock in his Electric Boat Company. Because he had incorporated what appeared to be non-productive submarine patents held by the Holland Torpedo Boat division into submarine contracts with Great Britain, the company's stock rose from $10 per share to $125. Rice sold 16,000 shares in July of 1915 for $2 million. Had he held them until the following October, he would have profited $16 million.[2] But his shrewd business sense prevented him from going bankrupt as had happened to so many others at this time. The submarine division of his Electric Boat Company was destined to make him a wealthy man.

With Rice's takeover of the Holland company came the $200,000 appropriation for the navy's first submarine that had been awarded on March 3, 1893, and entered into on March 13, 1895. As the new owner, Rice retained the officers of the company: John Holland, manager, Charles Creecy, attorney representing the company's Washington's interests, and E. B. Frost, secretary-treasurer. The latter was destined to become the overlord of the enterprise.[3] The company began the construction of the *Plunger*, the eighty-five-foot, steam-driven monster that was beset with problems from the start. Besides its "intimate fraternization" with the dock mentioned earlier, the submarine ran afoul when the engines were started for the first time. The craft was overpowered. The result was that she "almost turned turtle" when the gears were engaged.

Holland's illness during this period had prevented him from supervising the construction. The work was assigned to two inexperienced naval engineers, who seemed to be more occupied with incorporating the "improvements" suggested by navy brass than adhering to Holland's blueprints. Upon his recuperation and subsequent examination of the boat, John Holland knew that the submarine would never operate the way he had envisioned. What occurred between him and Frost has not been recorded, but he must have made the pending failure of the *Plunger* known to the secretary-treasurer. Frustrated, Holland began designing the smaller submarine *Holland* and was granted permission by company officials to build it without navy interference.[4]

The naval contract of 1893 strengthened the company's stock and permitted the generation of funds to construct the *Holland* under private contract. The craft took shape during the winter of 1896–97 in the Nixon's Crescent Shipyard in Elizabethport, New Jersey. On March 11, 1897, the small submarine made her maiden underwater voyage. The previous year Rice and Frost had been involved in government negotiations that were to set the stage for future congressional hearings on submarine monopolies. The outcome of their wheeling and dealing was the awarding of a second government appropriation of $350,000 to construct two additional submarines of the Plunger type. This created a unique situation for the Electric Boat Company. The first appropriation, of $200,000, had provided for the company's construction and experimentation with its first submarine. The *Plunger* was, for all intents and purposes, dead in the water. This was the reason Holland began the private construction of the company's second submarine, the *Holland*. Recognizing that the *Plunger* was doomed to failure and that they had better chances of success with the *Holland*, Rice and Frost were able to convince the navy to cancel the contract for the *Plunger* (April 11, 1900) and substitute the phrase "two boats of the *Holland* type," into the new contract, hoping the navy would also purchase the *Holland*. The company refunded the $94,364.68 paid to it by the government for work on the *Plunger*. Interestingly, Frost's accounting for the *Plunger* includes $89,730 for partial payment of the craft, $1,800 for two bow torpedo tubes, $1,500 for an air compressor, and $1,334.68 for advertising.[5] The situation that had developed was nicely summed up by R. G. Skerrett in his letter to the editor of *Scientific American* in 1908:

> As the "Plunger" progressed, the John P. Holland Torpedo Boat Company was paid successive installments of the contract price, and these part payments not only constituted reimbursement for the cost of construction, but included the profit the contractors expected to make. After more than five years of delayed construction—during which time the boat had served the profitable commercial end of stock selling and advertising—she was utterly abandoned, and the money paid out by the government was in effect refunded. The John P. Holland Torpedo Boat Company imposed as a condition that it should receive a new contract for a vessel of later design but of about half of the promised accomplishments of the original "Plunger" and at a cost of $20,000 more. By this arrangement, the interest on the ninety-odd thousand dollars paid out during that time went as so much profit to the Holland Company, and not a word was said about paying to the government the $80,000 in penalties due for the delay which had accrued against the "Plunger" during the five years of her building. By the contract, the "Plunger" was to have been completed within twelve months from the date her contract was signed.
>
> In 1896, the Holland interests secured the passage of a bill providing for the construction of two boats of the Holland design, in case the "Plunger" should prove a success; but at the time of passage of that bill the keel of the "Plunger" had not even been laid. The John P. Holland Torpedo Boat Company recognized that it could not hope to profit by that appropriation if the "Plunger" were to be depended upon to that end; and ac-

cordingly, later in 1896, they began the construction of that modest little craft since known as the "Holland."

It was not until 1898, however, that this small boat was able to maneuver with the required measure of certainty and security; and it was not until 1899 that she was able to meet the indulgent requirements outlined by the Department with due regard to the modest possibilities of that particular vessel.

This is what Mr. E. B. Frost, the secretary of the company, has said regarding the reasons for the building of the "Holland." His letter is dated April 28, 1900, and was addressed to the Hon. Eugene Hale, chairman of the Senate Committee on Naval Affairs:

"The company found after a year's work upon the "Plunger" that she could not be made to bring out the highest developments of the art, and therefore determined to build the "Holland" at its own expense which embodies the inventor's most advanced ideas. The success of the "Holland" has shown the wisdom of the company in this respect."[6]

It appears that the Electric Boat Company also demonstrated a good deal of financial wisdom in its dealings with the government. On April 11, 1900, the navy purchased the *Holland* for $150,000. The Holland Torpedo Boat Company estimated that the actual cost of the submarine was $236,615. Skerrett has tabulated the "bargain" the government really received for its investment:

	Promised 1893 Original "Plunger"	Realized 1899 "Holland"
Displacement submerged	138.5 tons	74 tons
Propelled by	3 screws	1 screw
Speed when light	15 knots	5.3 knots
Speed awash	14 knots	4.73 knots
Speed when submerged	8 knots	4 knots
Time to submerge completely from light condition	1 minute	16 minutes
Number of torpedo tubes	2	1
Provision for escape of crew	some	none

Upon the basis of total submerged displacement—$150,000 being the contract price for the "Plunger" as well as the price of the "Holland"—the "Plunger" was to cost $1,083 a ton, while the "Holland" actually cost not less than $2,027 a ton. As the table shows, the government paid a very tidy figure for "the inventor's most advanced ideas."[7]

The Holland Company was to build a second craft to replace the failed *Plunger.* Referred to as the *New Plunger,* the submarine was built to the same specifications as the *Holland* and paid for from the 1893 appropriation.[8] Rice and Frost knew their business well; on June 7, 1900, another appropriation was made for five additional submarines of the Holland type, not to exceed $170,000 each. The two industrialists had managed to convince naval officials to alter the wording of the contract, replacing the word *Plunger* with *Holland* and, in essence, replacing the model of submarine being built. This monopolistic headlock that the Holland Company was maintaining on the government began to concern a number of informed individuals in Washington. Rear Admiral George E. Wells testified that he considered $70,000 a reasonable price for the *Holland* rather than the $150,000 paid. Francis T. Bowles, chief constructor of the U.S. Navy, stated: "My calculations show that a reasonable cost, with a handsome profit to the contractor for the boats now building ("Adder" and class of 122 tons submerged displacement) would be $89,459. The government would pay $170,000 each for the five submarines of the *Adder* class, a sum of $850,000."[9]

Amid increasing public awareness of Electric Boat's undertakings, internal problems were also developing. This became apparent when the disgruntled man who preceded John Holland as president, Captain W. H. Jaques, threatened to expose the names of naval personnel for whom Frost was holding stock in trust. Apparently, when the Holland Company had been absorbed into Electric Boat, Captain Jaques did not receive what he considered to be his fair share of Electric Boat stock. Through a series of masterful legal maneuvers, Frost was able to prevent an investigation of these activities.[10] Satirically and seemingly to address Electric Boat's attitude at the time, the American cartoonist Joseph Thompson McAllister took the now famous photograph of John Holland emerging from the conning tower of his submarine and drew the first "What? Me worry?" cartoon.[11] In the years to come, Electric Boat would have a great deal to worry about.

Meanwhile, with the founding of the Lake Torpedo Boat Company in Bridgeport, Connecticut, Simon Lake had made the fateful decision to

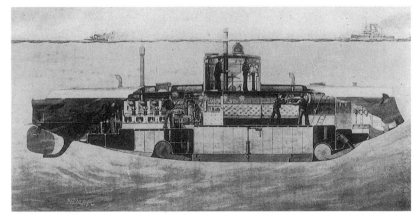

fig. 17. Internal view of the *Protector.* From Lake Torpedo Boat Company, *Under Water Torpedo Boats* (Bridgeport, Conn.: Lake Torpedo Boat Company, 1906)

enter the field of military submarine construction. This event would set the stage for major clashes with the Electric Boat Company. Lacking governmental support, Lake's company was on its own to build the submarine that would become Lake's *Protector.* This decision was largely based upon a request made of him by Senator Eugene Hale, chairman of the Senate Naval Committee, in 1901. Hale was aware of Lake's success with the *Argonaut* and considered the salvage craft applicable to harbor defense once certain design modifications were made in her.[12]

The *Protector* was launched November 1, 1902, at Bridgeport, Connecticut, and was designed to be a direct competitor with the Holland submarines. She was sixty-five feet in length, with an eleven-foot beam, and displaced 170 tons. Surface propulsion consisted of two screws driven by two gasoline engines of 250 horsepower and 100 horsepower electric motors for submerged running. The craft was capable of a surface speed of eleven knots and a submerged speed of seven knots. Her crew of six could spend an estimated submergence time of sixty hours in the comfort of quarters that resembled a sleeping car on American trains of the period. The submarine could operate at depth of 150 feet and had a cruising radius of one thousand miles with a submerged radius of fifty miles. Present on the submarine were Lake's characteristic wheels for bottom running, hydroplanes for even-keel diving, and his diver's chamber for clearing mines and cutting cables. Lake had also added one of his new inventions, called the "omniscope," a periscope that surpassed the primitive versions of the sighting devices being used on other submarines. The hull of the

Protector had a ship shape rather than the typical cigar shape—lessons learned from the *Argonaut*.[13]

During the *Protector's* construction, Lake and other company officials were doing their share of politicking in Washington in an attempt to break the Electric Boat Company's monopoly on government submarines. It was also during this period that Lake made his first trip to Europe on the invitation of several countries interested in his expertise. Russia was particularly interested and put out its red carpet to the inventor and his wife. Lake spent a great deal of time with Russian naval officials and, when not discussing submarines, had the opportunity to dine and attend the opera with Czar Nicholas. When Margaret Lake became ill, Nicholas sent his personal physician to care for her. Meanwhile, back home, things in Washington were beginning to heat up.[14]

With the *Protector* completed, the Lake Torpedo Boat Company approached the U.S. Navy about the possibility of trials for its newest submarine. The following account differs from that provided in various histories prepared by the Electric Boat Company and is based upon congressional hearings and the personal correspondence between Simon Lake and Lake Torpedo Boat Company officials. The circuitous path these industrial and political intrigues take requires that certain information be presented out of chronological order for the reader to gain a more complete understanding of the events.

In 1908, the House Select Committee under House Resolution 288 investigating submarine construction was initiated. Alleged corrupt practices were cited by Congressman George Lilly, later governor of Connecticut. In his opening statement, Lilly professed, "This Electric Boat Company has been a stench in the nostrils of the country for years, and, in my opinion, it has done more to corrupt legislation than all the other corporations on earth." He then made the following charges:

> I propose to show that for several years prior to the Lessler investigation the Holland Company, and its successor, the Electric Boat Company, maintained in Washington an organized lobby for the purpose of influencing legislative appropriations in favor of the Holland boat, and that it had under annual retainer C. E. Creecy, Gen. Eppa Hunton, ex-United States Senator Marion Butler, C. S. McNeir, Dr. W. R. Kerr, and others.
>
> That for several years Mr. Elihu B. Frost, vice-president of the said company, has been a continuous visitor at Washington during Congressional sessions, and that he has spent large sums

of money in furnishing entertainment to Members of Congress, and that his expenditures along this line amount to thousands of dollars.

That the Senate amendment to the appropriation bill of March 2, 1907, was prepared and drafted by the attorney for the Electric Boat Company for the purpose of and with the intention to eliminate competition in submarine construction, and to prevent the Secretary of the Navy from exercising any discretion in awarding contracts for submarines.

That a thorough investigation by an impartial committee will show that large sums of money have been, by the Electric Boat Company, its officers, or agents, contributed to campaign funds of Members of Congress who favor and have favored the Electric Boat Company's monopoly of submarine construction; also, that large sums of money have been spent to accomplish the defeat of members of the Naval Committee who did not favor the Electric Boat Company.

That an examination of the books and records of the Electric Boat Company and its predecessor, the Holland Boat Company, will show that large sums of money have been paid from their treasuries for the above purpose.

That continued and repeated efforts have been made by representatives of the Electric Boat Company and its predecessor to influence the action of the officials of the Navy department, and that such efforts in the past were so persistent and notorious as to call forth the condemnation and criticism of high officials of the Navy Department, whose testimony can be secured by an investigation committee.

That from 1893 up to the present time these efforts of the Electric Boat Company and the Holland Company have resulted in absolutely suppressing any possibility of competition in submarine construction, and securing and awarding of all contracts, either by specific appropriations or by legislative appropriations skillfully drawn, to this company without possibility of competition.

That it can be shown by former investigation before the Naval Committee of the House, upon which no reports were made to the House of Representatives that the Holland Company and the Electric Boat Company have been engaged in doubtful and reprehensible efforts to influence Members of Congress and officials of the Navy Department in favor of their boats and appropriations therefore.

That it can be shown upon investigation that certain representatives of leading newspapers have been subsidized and paid by the Electric Boat Company for favorable newspaper articles and reports in behalf of the said company.

It has never been held that evidence should be taken or submitted in advance to warrant Congressional investigation. Such a procedure would be investigation per se by the committee rules. . . . If these things are not actually within the pale of the law, they are wrongful practices and tend to throw discredit upon the Congress of the United States.[15]

Part of the impetus for the 1908 hearing was the result of an earlier Congressional action that became known as the Lessler investigation. During this 1903 investigation, Philip Doblin was found guilty of bribery and perjury for offering money to Congressional members in exchange for their vote favoring the awarding of contracts to the Electric Boat Company. Doblin had worked as a staff member on Congressman Lessler's campaign for reelection. It was a case of guilt by association. Fortunately for Lessler, he was not implicated in the bribery scandal, but the resulting hullabaloo served to focus attention on the antics of the Electric Boat Company. The pending submarine bill was passed without provisions for Electric Boat.

Although Lilly was unable to provide the proof necessary to support his allegations stated in House Resolution 288, the hearing brought to light the fact that all was not right in Washington.[16] The events leading up to this hearing involved Simon Lake's attempt to break Electric Boat's monopoly on submarine construction. His initial thrust came while his company was completing construction of the *Protector* in 1902. Through Representative E. J. Hill of Connecticut, Lake introduced a petition that resulted in the modification of language used in naval appropriations to include a competition between *existing* government submarines and those of *any* American inventor. This set the stage for a contest between the Lake Torpedo Boat Company and Electric Boat. It is noted in the background statements of House Resolution 288 that "[t]he rivalry between these two companies has not been simply a business rivalry between two manufacturing corporations. It has been a rivalry between jealous inventors, keen financiers, accomplished promoters of international fame, shrewd political agents, and resourceful lawyers."[17]

The word "competition" must have caused some disdain within the ranks of the Electric Boat Company. They had received the first governmental appropriation in 1895 to build the *Plunger*. A second noncompetitive appropriation was awarded them a year later for construction of two submarines of the *Plunger* type provided that their first craft be accepted by the Department of the Navy. When the Holland people realized that their first craft was a failure, they "convinced" naval authorities to purchase the smaller *Holland* and to alter the terms of the contract to read, "two submarines of the *Holland* type." The contract for the *Plunger* was canceled. The purchase of the *Holland* was definitely influenced by the favorable testimony of Admiral George Dewey, a monumental personality from the Spanish-American War. Dewey maintained that, had the Spanish employed two submarines of the *Holland's* caliber during the war, his entire squadron of fifteen ships would have been held at bay, unable to invade Manilla Bay.[18] The Electric Boat Company was awarded still a third contract for the construction of submarines on the strength of Dewey's statements. These submarines were to be of the Adder Class, whose contract was based solely upon the performance of the *Holland*. This class included the *Adder, Grampus, Moccasin, Pike, Porpoise,* and *Shark,* five submarines built at a profit of 410 percent.[19]

In addition to these successful negotiations with the U.S. government, the Electric Boat Company was also negotiating with Britain for submarines when a problem developed that would threaten their monopoly. Simon Lake had entered the military submarine market. The Holland people recognized that this would mean a direct competition between Lake's *Protector* and the Adder Class submarines. Secretary of the Navy William Henry Moody also foresaw the problem and summoned his senior member of the Board of Inspection and Survey, Captain C. J. Train. The latter, who was familiar with Lake's entry, opposed the competition, stating: "It is absolutely useless; I am ready to admit now that the 'Protector' outclasses anything which the government has."[20] The Electric Boat Company began building *Fulton* to counter this situation and prevent the disruption of its monopoly. The *Fulton* was an experimental boat designed not for the navy but specifically to compete with Lake's *Protector*.

What happened next is reminiscent of a nineteenth-century melodrama. On June 1, 1903, the Lake Company notified the secretary of the navy that it was ready for the competition. The navy hesitated in its reply for almost two months, finally acknowledging Lake's letter and indicating that the *Protector* would be tested against the *Fulton* (not one of the navy's commissioned submarines) on or about October 15, provided the *Fulton* could be presented on this date. The navy had effectively generated a three-plus month delay in the competition to the benefit of the Electric Boat Company. The preliminary tests of the first two Adder boats (*Adder* and *Moccasin*) were going poorly and reflecting badly upon the Electric Boat Company. Under no circumstances would the company employ either of these boats in the competition. More significantly to the trials, the *Fulton* had suffered a major setback when, in April of 1902, the submarine had been laid up after a destructive and nearly fatal explosion. The Electric Boat Company used this accident to further delay the competition, claiming nondelivery of materials necessary for repair and *improvements*. Then in December, like many of her Holland predecessors, the *Fulton* sank at her dock. The delays requested by the company were approved by the Navy Department despite the fact that the *Protector* had been ready for examination since June. To further harass the Lake Company, two lawsuits for patent infringements were filed by Electric Boat.

Lawrence Spear had resigned from the navy and was appointed vice president and naval architect of the Electric Boat Company. Much to the chagrin of John Holland, Spear had now replaced the inventor as the lead constructor. This action relegated Holland to the position of figurehead. Spear then worked closely with his friend U.S. Naval Constructor J. J. Woodward (the officer who had been charged with organizing and running the navy's competition) to set the rules and sequence of the competition's trials.[21]

While Lake waited for the competition, he had opportunity to entertain a number of individuals on the *Protector*. President Theodore Roosevelt's family, who were enjoying a vacation on the presidential yacht, were permitted to tour his submarine. More importantly to Simon Lake was the visitation by Major Arthur Murray, chief of the Coast Artillery Corps, and Captains Charles J. Bailey and Charles F. Parker. They were members of an army board that had been sent by Secretary of War William Howard Taft to inspect the *Protector*. The outcome of this meeting and several demonstration runs on the submarine was that the army decided to buy the *Protector* for $250,000. It also desired to purchase five more submarines of the Lake design. Fear struck the Electric Boat Company, and the Holland political machine went into high gear. Company officials approached the army, offering to build two submarines for a cost less than the single *Protector*. Their letter also included a lengthy discussion of the inferiority of the Lake type of submarine. These meetings may have had an impact. Although the army's appropriation for the Lake submarines was approved by the Senate, it was defeated in the House. Naval officials, under the guise of being responsible for all naval craft, had managed to bring sufficient pressure to bear upon House members to defeat the bill. Lake had won the battle of recognition but would lose the war for the immediate sale of his craft to the government.

At this point, it is necessary to jump ahead in this story to point out that both the *Protector* and the *Fulton* were eventually sold to Russia, who wanted to test both types of submarines. The Russian government had more experience with underwater craft than any other nation up to this time. After extensive tests, the *Protector* was deemed the best craft, and Lake received a second and then a third order for additional submarines from the Russian government. Electric Boat Company officials, meanwhile, sought other markets and began plying their wares in Europe, particularly in England. In retrospect, recognition of the superiority of the Lake submarine had been provided by Captain Train of the U.S. Navy, by Major Murray of the U.S. Army, and also by members of the Russian Navy. Yet acceptance of the Lake submarine by naval officials in the United States would have to await changes in the administration.

The *Protector* was taken from Bridgeport to Newport, Rhode Island, unescorted and during a severe storm, for the trials set for November 17, 1903. One of her engines broke down and required that the boat be put in dry dock. The trials had to be canceled. Lake found that the propellers he had used were not giving the submarine her proper speed. The original props provided a speed of 10.65 knots while the replacements reduced its maximum speed to 8 knots. He realized that this would disqualify her and requested that the Naval Board test the boat and give exception to its low speed. In a letter to the department he indicated that if such consideration were given, the company would make the necessary adjustments to correct the problem. Immediately, a vehement protest was raised by Naval Constructor Woodward. He attempted to force Lake into signing a statement declaring the results of the trials final and that he would waive all rights to further trials. Lake refused. Woodward then insisted that the trial begin. There would be no side-by-side competition since the *Fulton* was in repair. On January 12, 1904, the *Protector* was taken into Narragansett Bay accompanied by the navy tug *Powhatan* and the yacht *Hist,* which was to be used as an observation platform for the board of examiners. The ice flows were so heavy that the president of the Board of Inspection and Survey insisted on canceling the trial even though the *Protector* made her run over the prescribed mile-long course. The submarine returned to the Naval Torpedo Station without incident. Despite the fact that the course was clear the following day, the board decided to postpone the trial indefinitely.

Lake was still concerned about the statement Woodward had insisted he sign regarding the finality of the trials. He requested that the board meet the next day, at which time Lake's lawyer from New York would be available to discuss the statement. They arrived at the hotel where the board members were staying. Naval Constructor Woodward promptly left on the first train out of Newport, effectively blocking the presentation of Lake's case. The rest of the board did not depart until late in the afternoon. Woodward had also dictated to the board not only the scope of the trials but also the character and manner of test, as discussed with Electric Boat vice president Spear. When Lake finally contacted Woodward to discuss the legalities of the trial, Woodward's reply was: "Congress can make the laws, but I propose to interpret it as I see fit."[22] In considering Woodward's actions, Robert Skerrett wrote:

> It is only airing the Naval Department's dirty linen to discuss at length the many ways in which Naval Constructor Woodward obstructed the intent of Congress and perverted official authority to the injury of the Lake Torpedo Boat Company; but it is only fair to the American people, and to those officers of the American Navy, whose first aim is the honor and welfare of the service, that the action of the Navy Department may be centered on the evil genius who is responsible, not only for driving an American enterprise abroad for consideration, but also who is responsible for the deliberate perversion of the intent of Congress, and directly responsible for the many thousands of dollars that have been spent since in a vain effort to make the submarines in the United States Navy something like as efficient and as safe as the Lake Torpedo Boat Company's "Protector" was even at the time the Board of Inspection and Survey refused to continue her trials in January of 1904.[23]

By 1904, the delaying tactics of the Navy Board were creating a financial drain on the Lake Torpedo Boat Company. Lake's earlier trip to Russia had resulted in negotiations for four million dollars in submarines. The outbreak of the Russo-Japanese War in 1904 strengthened Russia's need to purchase the *Protector*. Lake agreed to the sale because of the financial difficulties his company was facing. Within a week of learning that the *Protector* was being dismantled for shipment to Russia, the Electric Boat Company's *Fulton* was declared ready for trials by the navy. Interestingly, Electric Boat now had on its hands an expensive experimental boat, the *Fulton,* that had not been contracted for by the U.S. Government. Subsequently, the *Fulton* was also sold to Russia (after the navy trials). It appears that the Russians may have been suspicious of the navy's trials and wanted to make their own comparison of the two American submarines.[24]

The *Fulton* had finally shown up for its trial after eleven months of preparation. The navy's tests on her were held between June 1 and 10, 1904, and Constructor Woodward quickly passed on the results, indicating that the *Fulton* fulfilled all of the stated requirements set forth by the naval board. This rapid approval was necessary because the $500,000 appropriation pending in Congress was set to run out on June 20, 1904. Additionally, and prior to this expiration, Congress increased the appropriation to $850,000, ordering four additional submarines. This turn of events made the contract all the more enticing to the Electric Boat Company. But all was not rosy for the company. During the sea trials of the *Porpoise* (one of the submarines completed by the Electric Boat for the navy), the pilot lost control of the craft and could not pull it out of a steep dive. The nose of the submarine buried itself in the bottom mud of Narragansett Bay 125 feet below the surface. It was a harrowing experience for the crew, especially when they contemplated a much heralded experiment by the Holland Company. The company had demonstrated a method of submarine escape in which a dog was shot from one of the torpedo tubes. This experiment had been undertaken as a deliberate attempt to discredit the value of Lake's diver's chamber that could double as an escape hatch. If the situation in the sunken submarine had not been so serious, the Holland escape plan would have been laughable as the torpedo tubes were buried three to four feet in the mud. The sub was finally freed from the bottom through heroic efforts. But the accident caused a considerable amount of dismay in Washington with respect to the diving type of submarine.[25]

Another facet of the naval trials came to light a few years later, after the Russian government had completed its comparative tests of the *Protector* and the *Fulton*. The Russian report, which declared the *Protector* the superior boat and resulted in a substantial contract for the Lake Company in Russia, was kept from the Navy Department by Constructor Woodward.[26]

Lake was by this time working in Europe, primarily in Russia, but also dealing with the German, Austrian, and British governments. Still wanting to break the Electric Boat Company monopoly on submarines, he ordered his company to begin construction of another submarine to be used in future government competitions. The *Simon Lake X* (i.e., number 10), was beset with problems from the start. There was an attempt to incorporate improvements learned from the company's experience with the *Protector*. With Lake in Europe and unable to supervise his engineers, many of the improvements proved faulty. To compound the problem, a rather suspicious event occurred. The *Lake* was docked near the Stratford Avenue Bridge in Bridgeport, Connecticut. She was held to the dock by hawsers and ropes that had been made fast to the tender Vesta. During the darkened hours of February 10, 1908, vandals thoroughly familiar with the submarine opened sea valves, and the *Lake* began to take on water. The crew of the *Vesta* was awakened when the tender began to list under the submarine's weight. The valves were quickly shut, but not until $22,000 worth of damage had occurred. Pinkerton detectives were unable to identify the vandals, and many people began to suspect industrial espionage. Some believed that the partial sinking had been the result of carelessness on the part of the crew. A few began to think that Simon Lake might be suffering from paranoia. The latter might have appeared to be the case because a valve left open could very well have been accidental (much like what had happened to a number of the early Holland boats); however, when it was discovered that *four* valves were opened, the case for paranoia quickly dissipated.[27]

During 1906, officers of the Lake Torpedo Boat Company were able to convince naval officials of the need for another competition between their most advanced submarines and the *Simon Lake X*. The governmental trials for the *Lake* took place in May of 1907 at Newport, Rhode Island. The Lake craft was pitted against the newest Electric Boat Company submarine, the *Octopus*. The *Lake* was no match for the *Octopus* in terms of speed, and the Lake boat even had difficulties diving on an even keel. Simon Lake's absence during the construction had serious consequences for the company and its desire to obtain a contract form the U.S. government. The appropriation for seven submarines again went to the Electric Boat Company. However, Secretary of the Navy Victor H. Metcalf became convinced the the Lake Company could produce military craft possessing distinct merits, though he felt obliged to leave the question regarding the awarding of submarine contracts to Attorney General Charles Bonapart. The Attorney General rendered the opinion that the navy could, in fact, contract the Lake firm for one of its submarines. The catch was that the company would have to foot the expense of the construction and no governmental funds would be expended for her until the boat was approved and accepted by the navy. Once again, and unlike the government's treatment of Electric Boat, the Lake Torpedo Boat Company was on its own to build a submarine for the U.S. Government.[28]

As a footnote to this chapter, another aspect of the dealings of the Electric Boat Company needs to be presented. It comes in the form of a letter from John P. Holland to C. E. Foss, chairman of the Committee on Naval Affairs in 1906. Portions of the letter read:

I am the inventor of the Holland submarine boat, now in use in the United States Navy, and in Europe. My old patents, to the number of about twenty, are owned by the Electric Boat Company. On June 16th, 1900, I entered into a contract with that company, to serve as their engineer for five years, dating back to April 1st, 1899, and expired April 1st 1904. Since the expiration of my contract with the Electric Boat Company, I have devoted myself to remedying the defects in my old inventions, and perfecting designs, by which the low speed of the present Holland boats can be increased three or four times. . . . I procured the organization of a company—"John P. Holland's Submarine Boat Company," May 18th, 1905, with sufficient capital to build a boat under my plans and inventions, and was about to start work, when the Electric Boat Company filed a suit against me in the Court of Chancery of New Jersey, applying for an injunction, and claiming substantially that I had agreed to assign to them all my inventions and patents during the term of my natural life. Two other suits have been started, one against my new company in the United States Circuit Court to enjoin the use of the name "Holland," the other, against me personally, a verbal contract never to compete with the Electric Boat Company, was commenced in the New Jersey Court of Chancery. . . . These suits have had the effect of frightening off the capital that I had enlisted, and I have not as yet been able to get the capital to build my new boat, by reason of these suits. The only object of these suits was to prevent me from building a boat and going into competition before the Navy Department with the submarine boats now being built by the Electric Boat Company under my old patents. . . . My attention has been called to the bill (H.R. 10070), entitled "A bill to increase the efficiency of the Navy." It must be apparent to every member of your Committee that this bill is drawn solely in the interest of the Electric Boat Company monopoly. . . . I hardly think, Mr. Chairman, that your Committee, in making an appropriation for submarine boats, will exclude the Navy Department from any consideration of plans made by me, when I say to you that these plans have the approval of some of the most expert officers in the

Navy on the question of submarine boats, and that the boats
can be built at one-third less than is now being paid the Electric
Boat Company for boats two-thirds less submerged and more
than fifty percent less surface speed. . . . I am a poor man, while
the Electric Boat Company has among its principal stockholders
three or four millionaires, including August Belmont, Isaac
Rice, and others. The capital stock of that Company is ten million dollars. They have deprived me, by their flimsy lawsuit,
from getting capital to build a boat under my new inventions
and patents, and are now asking Congress to pass a law which
will prevent the Navy Department from adopting my new plans
and inventions should the entire Department consider that they
are far superior in every way to the plans now being used by the
Department. . . . I do not believe that your Committee will com-
mit itself to this monopoly which is against the interests of the
Government.[29]

The Electric Boat Company had turned against the man responsible
for their success and was now depriving him of any monetary rewards for
his patents. It was applying the same tactics against John Holland that it
had used against Simon Lake when he tried to break Electric Boat's monopoly on submarine construction.

CHAPTER 6

Off to Europe

*A*merica invents while Europe capitalizes.
—*Nineteenth-century inventors' adage*

The first decade of the twentieth century was an exuberant, exhilarating, and romantic period. It was the time of Rudyard Kipling, Thomas Mann, Horatio Alger, Jack London, Anton Dvoÿrák, and Maurice Ravel. Ragtime jazz developed in America, and the Cake Walk was the fashionable dance of the day. Leon Trotsky escaped from a Siberian prison and had settled in London, while Rasputin was gaining influence in the Russian court. The negotiations for the Panama Canal had just been completed and Theodore Roosevelt's "big hole" would soon become a reality. Guglielmo Marconi transmitted the first telegraph message across the Atlantic, and Reginald Aubrey Fessenden extended this accomplishment by transmitting the human voice over radio waves. Albert Einstein formulated the theory of relativity, and Orville and Wilbur Wright successfully flew a powered airplane. Henry Ford founded the Ford Motor Company, while J. P. Morgan organized his International Mercantile Marine Company. The Age of Steam was now being replaced by the Age of Electricity. The Spanish-American War, referred to as "that splendid little war" by Secretary of State John Hay, had ended, resulting in a strong nationalistic spirit for the United States as an up-and-coming world power. An invigorated, flag-waving patriotism was very evident in the country. Business was booming and industry was becoming supreme. In preparing the history of General Dynamics, the mammoth corporation that was to absorb the Electric Boat Company, the authors made a rather interesting statement about this period: "Since industry was clearly bringing benefits to the American people, it was easy to confuse industry (and exploitation, and monopoly, and relentless competition) with the benefits themselves. Even some of the ministry caught the contagion, and left behind sermons that did not clearly differentiate between God and Mammon."[1]

The pace of submarine innovation had also quickened. The work of men like Bushnell, Hunley, and Fulton had provided the impetus for the refinement of the submarine as a major instrument of war. With his entrance into the construction of military submarines and his unsuccessful attempt to sell the *Protector* to the U.S. Government, Simon Lake was forced to seek other markets. His first trip to Russia in 1902 resulted in a five-year contract for submarine construction totaling $4 million. The saber rattling between Russia and Japan that would lead to the Russo-Japanese War in February of 1904 had increased Russia's desire for submarines. Ironically, Lake had almost sold the *Protector* to the Japanese. He had engaged the services of Charles R. Flint, a prominent New York banker who was also a promoter, former diplomat, and, above all, dealer in munitions. Flint was aware of the dual interest in the *Protector* of the Russians and the Japanese and favored the former, probably for business reasons. Flint's representative in Europe, Hart O. Berg, had convinced the Russians to purchase the Lake boat. Lake was to meet with the Japanese legation in Washington, but Flint sidetracked him into meeting with the Russians first, keeping him occupied most of the day to prevent any contact with the Japanese. The Russian naval attaché provided authorization from the J. P. Morgan Company to pay the $125,000 needed to bind the purchase of the *Protector.* The balance of the $250,000 pricetag was to be paid upon satisfactory performance of the submarine in Russia. Lake felt bad about not meeting with the Japanese representative. Flint responded by requesting one of Lake's business cards. Handing it to his secretary, he told him to go to the hotel where the Japanese representative was staying and, after making sure he was not in his room, to slip the card under his door. Flint had written on the card, "Sorry I missed you."[2]

Foster M. Voorhees, vice president of the Lake Torpedo Boat Company, was a close friend of former secretary of war Benjamin F. Tracy. The former secretary indicated to both Lake and Voorhees that shipping contraband to a foreign country violated the neutrality laws of the United States. He also warned that the company was certain to encounter Japanese resistance toward any attempt to ship the *Protector.* However, one way of side-stepping the neutrality laws was to transport war materials in an unfinished form. Lake had decided earlier to change the batteries in the *Protector* and saw this as an opportunity to send a "partial" submarine to Russia. Flint chartered the steamer *Fortuna* for this purpose under the guise of shipping a load of coal to Libau, Russia.

During the days that followed, the newspapers learned of the impending sale of the *Protector*. Lake and his company officers were under constant surveillance by reporters and Japanese officials. One Saturday morning, Lake set out for Newport from Bridgeport ostensibly to conduct further sea trials with the *Protector*. As the submarine began her run up Long Island Sound, a heavy fog set in and the submarine's course was changed for New York. He passed through Hell Gate around midnight and reached the harbor, where the giant derrick *Monarch* was ready with slings to hoist the *Protector* into its cradle on the deck of the *Fortuna* during the night. The *Fortuna*, however, did not arrive until eight o'clock Sunday morning, and the *Protector* had to be loaded in broad daylight in the view of pleasure craft cruising the harbor. Fortunately, nothing was reported of the rather strange Sunday-morning endeavor. Lake was now faced with a second problem. But this one was easily solved to his complete satisfaction. None of his crew had been told the real reason for the late-night escapade. All had packed small handbags with clothing and personal items for a three-day run on the *Protector*. Lake explained the *Protector*'s sale to Russia and asked for volunteers to make the trip to Europe. He was very pleased when every member of the crew raised his hand in an affirmative desire to accompany the *Protector* to its new home in Libau. He selected eight of the volunteers. It would be seven years before they would return home.[3]

To maintain the secrecy of the transport of the *Protector* to Russia, Lake returned to Bridgeport and remained there for several days in view of his stalkers. He then took a fast liner to Paris, where he met with the Russian ambassador. The Russians, notorious for their secrecy, requested Lake to travel under the assumed name of Elwood Simons. Only the Czar, the minister of marine, and certain higher naval officials were knowledgeable of this alias. It would be several months before he was allowed to use his own name. He would become known as Gospodin Semon to his Russian employees.

Lake was reunited with his crew in Kronstadt, near St. Petersburg, and learned that their veil of secrecy had been so complete that the officers of the Russian destroyers in the Baltic were unaware of the *Protector*'s delivery until her hull was recognized by the crew of a Russian destroyer as a submarine sitting atop the *Fortuna*'s deck. The *Fortuna*'s crew had made the mistake of removing the *Protector*'s canvas cover. Because the ship did

fig. 18. Lake submarines being shipped to Europe. From Lake Torpedo Boat Company, *Under Water Torpedo Boats* (Bridgeport, Conn.: Lake Torpedo Boat Company, 1906)

not slow to a speed acceptable to the destroyer's captain, she received a shot across her bow. A boarding crew was sent to the *Fortuna,* fearing that the *Protector* was being smuggled into Russia by the Japanese. Shortly thereafter, a second destroyer arrived and accompanied the *Fortuna* to Kronstadt. Once safely docked, the Russian Admiralty sanctioned Lake's arrival and the escort returned to patrolling the Baltic waters.[4]

Several of the Russian officers assigned to assist Lake in making his arrangements for the *Protector's* trials proudly pointed out the submarine *Delfin,* which had been built by the Russian Navy and was moored to its dock as the *Fortuna* steamed by. The *Delfin* had been built at the Baltic Works in St. Petersburg and was based upon the basic submarine design of John Holland. The Russians had thoroughly investigated Holland's work, and their naval attaché in Washington had made runs on both the *Holland* and *Fulton.* Although the attaché submitted a negative report on these craft, the Russian technical committee on submarines overrode the report and went forward with the construction of the *Delfin* based upon their knowledge of Holland's design. She was launched in 1903 and, from all accounts, was a very successful craft.[5] The officers of the *Delfin* told Lake that their submarine was being used to train Russian sailors, some of whom were to become the crew of the *Protector.* Their training usually began with dockside submergence exercises to familiarize the crew with the diving procedures. As Lake discussed submarines with the officers, dinner was served. During the meal, an orderly delivered a message to the captain heading up the naval contingent attending Lake and his crew. The captain's face paled as he read the message. Something had gone wrong during the *Delfin*'s dive, and twenty-eight of the thirty-five men on board had drowned. It was a terrible accident and may have served to strengthened the Russian conviction of the need for safety offered by the Lake boats. Amazingly, three of the *Delfin*'s survivors volunteered to train and serve on the *Protector*.

The acceptance trials of the *Protector* were held in the Gulf of Finland during the latter part of 1904. She was to be tested against the Electric Boat Company's *Fulton,* which had been shipped intact to Russia. The *Fulton* was captained by Frank Cable. Both he and Lake reported to the Russian naval commission that their submarines were ready for the trials. On the morning of the appointed day, Cable and his submarine did not appear. He indicated that he needed two additional days to clean his engines for the fifty-mile test run from Cronstadt to Bjorke. The *Protector* made the run alone. The *Fulton* appeared the next day, requiring a tow by a steamer to reach Bjorke and a barge fitted with a complete machine shop to keep her in operation. According to Lake, the trials of the *Fulton* were unsatisfactory.[6] However, Russia's need for submarines prompted the Naval Ministry to recommend purchasing the *Fulton* (renamed the *Som*) and order six additional Holland submarines—an order that, for unknown reasons, was delayed.[7]

The *Protector* met the requirements set by the Russian Naval Board, and Lake was rewarded with a five-year, $4 million contract. He was provided with a plant in Libau named the E. Simons Zavode, where five submarines (built and partially completed at the Newport News Shipbuilding Company in Virginia) were assembled and tested. These were the *Bychok* (Bullhead), *Kefal* (Gray Mullet), *Paltus* (Turbot or Halibut, depending upon translation), *Plotva* (Roach), and *Sig* (Salmon).[8] Shortly thereafter, an entire shipyard in St. Petersburg was turned over to him for the building of four large cruiser-type submarines.[9]

The Russians' experimentation with the *Protector* continued until it was decided to ship her six thousand miles overland for the protection of Vladivostok in the Far East. The region was threatened with invasion by the Japanese as the Russo-Japanese War was reaching its conclusion. Thanks to the Nobel Peace Prize–winning efforts of Theodore Roosevelt, negotia-

fig. 19. Lake submarines being transported across Russia to Vladivostok during the Russo-Japanese War. From Lake Torpedo Boat Company, *Under Water Torpedo Boats* (Bridgeport, Conn.: Lake Torpedo Boat Company, 1906)

tions eventually halted the war. Lake's submarine did not see battle. Had the conflict continued, an intriguing situation could possibly have developed. While Lake was building submarines for Russia, the Electric Boat Company had built and sold five Holland-type submarines to the Japanese. If Roosevelt had not intervened, the two types of submarines might have been put to the ultimate test, pitting one American-built submarine against the other in battle. The Russians felt that they had the advantage. The Russian officer who was put in charge of the *Protector* informed Lake that he could easily have sunk major portions of the Japanese fleet off Vladivostok had he not been ordered to refrain from attacking while the peace negotiations were in progress. The Japanese, with their Holland submarines, probably felt the same way.[10]

During this period, other submarine constructors were, for various reasons, having difficulties with submarine construction. Krupp of Germany had been unable to supply contracted submarines to either Russia or its own nation. Italy had also attempted to build a number of submarines but was unable to get them to function properly. The Electric Boat Company had built submarines for England, but these craft were beset with problems, as were their U.S. Navy counterparts. An Englishman's reply to an editorial in the *Army and Navy Journal* of June 24, 1905, provides some idea of the problems that submarine constructors were facing. His letter appeared shortly after the sinking of the Holland-type British submarine *A8:*

> The English and American [submarines] are the same type exactly. The only reason the English have more accidents is because the English Navy constantly uses its submarines in practice while the American are laid up for repairs most of the time and seldom used. Not a single United States submarine is in commission today. When you do use them the accidents are constant and dangerous. Specifically, I recall the explosions of the 'Fulton' and 'Porpoise,' the wrecks of the 'Adder,' 'Moccasin,' and 'Plunger,' and the terribly uncontrolled plunge of the 'Porpoise' and the 'Shark.' Just recently I noted the crew refused to go out for practice at San Francisco because of the danger. The United States did not lose lives because she towed the 'Adder,' 'Moccasin,' and the 'Plunger' empty, while the crew of the 'Porpoise' was saved by a miracle. The game is not worth the candle, and the trouble is the craft—not the brave men. I hope American fairness will prompt you to show the facts and not reflect on the ability of the brave and efficient sailors of the Royal Navy, who do the best possible with their 'sea coffins.' Togo did not use a single submarine, and yet the American builders of these craft attempt to fill the press with false reports of their worth in the Japan sea-fight. The press is responsible for the senseless submarine promotion to such an extent that some people wonder where the interest comes from.[11]

What also bothered many people in the United States was the assertion that Vickers and Maxim of England (who were responsible for construction of the Holland-type submarines in England) had actually gained controlling interest of the Electric Boat Company. Lake, who was still attempting to break Electric Boat's stronghold on the U.S. government, commented to Senator E. J. Hill of Connecticut:

> A gentleman who claims to have seen the Contract between the parties concerned is my authority for the above statement, and he tells me he will testify to that effect if called upon. I only mention this to show you that if it is true, . . . then the United States has already again placed herself in the hands of foreigners to whom she must go for further purchases and development of

this particular type of boat for the country's defense, and the
known facts would seem to bear this out, because every student
of submarine affairs knows that Vickers and Maxim are building
better boats for England today than the Electric Boat Company
is building for America; the result is that America is only permitted to follow rather than lead.[12]

A thorough study of the involvement of the Electric Boat Company with
Vickers and Maxim would undoubtedly prove interesting and should be
investigated, but this remains the theme for a future treatise dealing with
this segment of submarine history.

Through Hart O. Berg, Lake learned that Austria was interested in
building submarines. Emperor Franz Joseph had assigned Admiral Sieg-
fried Popper, minister of marine, to investigate the possibility of having
Lake build two submarines for his navy. Popper had designed a number
of submarines and was held in high regard by Lake for his nautical engineering skills. After seeing Lake's designs, Popper paid Lake his greatest
compliment, stating: "When I saw your plans I recognized that you had
introduced a number of valuable features that were better than mine, and
also that you had actual experience in building and operating submarines,
so I went to the Emperor and asked his consent to substitute your type
of boat for my own. . . . Do you know, Mr. Lake, I have been responsible
for the design of all other vessels built for the Austrian Navy during the
25 years?"[13]

The two submarines were completed to the satisfaction of the Austrian officials, and Lake now found himself in demand in other countries
of Europe. Krupp of Germany now wanted to construct Lake submarines.
He signed a lucrative contract for these rights. Lake was to a receive a
handsome consulting fee in addition to a royalty to the Lake Torpedo Boat
Company of 12 1/2 percent on all of Krupp's business with Russia, 6 percent on all boats built for Germany, and 7 1/2 percent on all submarines
Krupp built for Italy.

Lake's experiences in Germany were many and varied; some good,
many bad. For example, upon returning to his Berlin residence one day,
he found that his house had been searched by the police. It seems that a
man using the name Lake had committed a crime. Anyone bearing this
name was suspect. At the Criminal Courts Building, Lake learned that the
German police were looking for a counterfeiter. The perpetrator was apparently an American using the alias Samuel Lake who paid for his hotel
and restaurant bills with Confederate money. The police officials showed

Lake $250 in Confederate bills. It was the first Confederate money Lake had ever seen. One of the women who had been swindled was able to convince the police that Lake was not their man, and he was released. He never did learn the identity of the counterfeiter nor was he ever assessed of the outcome of the case.[14]

The experience in Germany that seemed to have its greatest effect upon Lake was his dealing with Admiral Alfred von Tirpitz. This German Navy admiral would have profound effects on the employment of submarines during World War I. The admiral had visited the United States to observe certain of the early *Holland* trials. Like many naval personnel of the time, he was not impressed. His disenchantment was summed up in this statement: "I am so sure that they are of no value that I won't even waste time experimenting with them."[15] Here, Lake's impact upon history becomes evident because, as his involvement with Krupp increased, the admiral's opinion of submarines changed significantly. Based upon Lake's designs for larger submarines, Tirpitz ceased viewing them as crude craft suitable only for coastal defense and began considering them as long-range, offensive weapons. Documenting Lake's contributions to the German submarine effort has been difficult. There is no doubt that Krupp was privy to Lake's most current designs and obviously used them in the construction of its submarines. Further, because Lake had inadvertently let his patent rights on a large number of his designs lapse, Germany felt free to employ them without remuneration to or recognition of Lake or his company. There is little doubt that many of Lake's submarine patents roamed the Atlantic during the First and Second World Wars in German submarines. Particularly troubling to Lake was Tirpitz's use of unrestricted submarine warfare during World War I. It was this tactic that drew the United States into the conflict, and Lake faced the realization that his designs were being used to sink Allied shipping.[16]

While working in Europe, Lake was required to make numerous trips back to the United States to oversee the submarine construction taking place at the Lake Torpedo Boat Company in Connecticut and the Newport News Ship Building Company in Virginia. This extensive travel was necessary for an additional reason. His company had arranged for another governmental competition to be held. His factory was busy constructing the *Lake X,* which was slated to be tested against one of the navy's submarines. As with the first competition between the Holland and Lake companies, political maneuvering ran rampant. A clause had been inserted in the naval appropriation act of March 3, 1903, authorizing the secretary of the navy to contract for submarines provided that competitive or comparative trials be held between any boats submitted by private owners and the best vessel owned by the government. The Electric Boat Company chose to enter its newest boat, the *Octopus,* which was not a government submarine but an experimental craft built specifically by the company to counter the threat of the *Lake X* to the Holland-type submarines then owned by the government. It was reminiscent of the *Fulton* fiasco. How it happened that this nongovernmental craft was permitted to compete against the Lake submission is still a mystery. The competition served to reopen old wounds, and the animosities between the two companies that resurfaced led to the Congressional hearing in 1908. The charges and countercharges brought out during this hearing revealed some interesting information. When Isaac Rice was asked if the Electric Boat Company was a strictly American-owned company, his reply was, "Purely." This caused a stir in the hearing because many of the participants were aware of Electric Boat's financial link with Vickers in England. When asked whether any company stock was owned by foreign interests, he would not reply, except to say that this information was "private." Rice indicated that he would provide this information to the committee in private, but there is no record that this was ever done.[17]

Although on the surface little appeared to have been accomplished by these hearings, the public washing of Electric Boat's laundry alleging political favoritism was to set the stage for the ultimate breakup of the company's monopoly on submarine construction. Lake and his company had paid dearly for the political shenanigans that were going on and also for Lake's long absences in supervising the construction of the craft that their hopes were pinned to. The *Lake X* made a terrible showing in the trials and, as in the past, the government contract was awarded to the Electric Boat Company.

Lake's transatlantic trips, often covering over seventeen thousand miles, had taken their toll upon his health. He became ill during a return voyage on the *Lusitania,* and the ship's doctor diagnosed the beginnings of a nervous breakdown. The physician's recommendation was complete rest. Following the doctor's orders, Lake rented a small cottage at Fort Trumbull in Milford, Connecticut, and remained there with his family until his health improved.

Upon his recovery, Lake returned to Europe to promote his submarine business. Electric Boat had numerous company representatives hawking their wares throughout Europe. This was not Lake's style. He felt personally responsible for his submarines and made the rounds of the various governments almost single-handedly. His travels brought him into contact with many of the significant historical events of the time. While in St. Petersburg, Russia, Hart O. Berg asked Lake to review a proposal that had been submitted to Charles Flint. Berg said, "Simon, here is a lot of stuff Flint has sent over. He has evidently got hold of another 'crazy inventor,' a man who thinks he can fly, and tells me he can get the European rights to this invention if we assist in financing the building of one of these flying machines."[18] The "crazy inventor" was Wilbur Wright. Lake had an interest in flight and would later patent a forerunner to the helicopter. He spent the better part of that evening reviewing the Wright patents and came to the conclusion that the brothers' claims were justifiable and that the plane would fly. He recommended to Berg that he contact Flint immediately and sign a contract with the brothers as their representative. Inadvertently, Lake did not ask to be a subscriber to their venture, a mistake he would later regret. Flint had requested that Lake permit the Wright brothers to use one of his offices as their European headquarters. Lake befriended Wilbur Wright and was able to witness one of the aviator's first flights at Le Mans, France.[19]

A little-known historical fact concerning Simon Lake's activities in Europe deals with his interest in tunnels. He had found time in 1906 to design a method for constructing long underwater tunnels and submitted his plans to both the English and French governments. These plans laid out a feasible way to construct a tunnel between England and the continent. However, political feelings at the time prevented its application. If Lake were alive today, he would obviously take pride in his contribution to the "Chunnel."[20]

As if the military submarine construction in Europe were not enough work for one man, Lake was called upon by Lloyds of London to consider salvaging the wreck of the *Lutine*. This vessel was a French frigate (captured by the British in 1793) that had been overhauled and recommissioned as part of the British fleet. In 1799, during a money panic in Germany, Britain decided to send funds to support its interests in Hamburg. On October 9, 1799, during a voyage from Yarmouth, England, to Hamburg, Germany, the *Lutine* sank in a violent storm. The ship went down in the Zuider Zee near Texel Reef off the coast of Holland, in seventy feet of water. She reportedly carried a large quantity of gold and silver specie (estimated to be worth six million dollars). For the next hundred years, the treasure was protected by the strong currents in the area, save for a limited amount of treasure salvaged by local fishermen. Lake could not resist the quest and began planning. He purchased the so-called *Lutine Bible* from Lloyds. This was a volume bound in a black oak cover and ornamented with copper from the ship, containing all of the pertinent information Lloyds could muster about the wreck. Its last sixty-eight pages were blank.[21]

Lake planned to employ one of his salvage tubes to retrieve the *Lutine* treasure. A large portion of the tube was completed in England when work on the *Lutine* project ceased. Changes in the navy's attitude toward the Lake-type submarine, coupled with the events in Europe that would lead to World War I, forced him to abandon his English tube and his plans to salvage the *Lutine*.

Positive attitudes concerning the submarine's role as an important adjunct to a naval fleet were developing in most of the world's navies. Submarine developments continued to advance in the United States. These craft were receiving support for a larger role in naval affairs by the White House. Theodore Roosevelt was president, and as a former secretary of the navy, he demonstrated his continuing interest in the navy's acquisition of underwater craft when, on August 26, 1905, he became the first U.S. president to go down in a submarine. The Electric Boat Company's new *Plunger* was said to require "work" in order to make it safe enough for the president of the United States to dive in her (a cost to the taxpayers that was over $30,000). Roosevelt made his short excursion in the *Plunger* and was so impressed with the hazards submariners were being subjected to that he authorized an immediate one-dollar increase in pay for every day a submariner spent underwater. It was the start of hazardous duty pay in the military services.[22]

As the first decade of the nineteenth century came to a close, Lake received notification that the U.S. Navy was again making a call for submarines. The congressional hearing of 1908, which had caused a good deal of concern in Washington with regard to the Electric Boat Company's monopoly on government submarine construction, had opened the door for new submarine constructors. The time seemed right for Lake to make one more try at gaining acceptance of his submarines by his government. Through the efforts of numerous individuals, particularly Governor Hill of Connecticut and Attorney General Bonapart, the Lake Torpedo Boat Company would produce its first submarine for the United States. The Electric Boat Company's monopoly had finally been broken.

CHAPTER 7

Half a Submarine

A war regarded as inevitable or even probable, and
therefore much prepared for, has a very good chance
of eventually being fought.
                                    —*George Frost Kennan*

From a naval standpoint, the First World War would mark the
advent of the submarine as a practical weapon of war.[1] The advances in underwater technology between 1898 and 1914 had increased both the range and endurance of submarines, extending
their military value from mere coastal defense craft to more rug-
ged seagoing leviathans. Early submarines (ca. 1900) were considered
primitive and unreliable, measuring some sixty feet in length and capable
of surface speeds of eight to nine knots. Underwater, their speed was reduced to four to five knots. By the outbreak of the war in 1914, submarines
had grown to more efficient craft measuring 170 plus feet in length, with
surface speeds of 15 1/2 knots and submerged speeds of 9 1/2 knots. These
developments initiated changes in naval thinking regarding the role submarines could play in naval engagements, but what seemed to spur this
attitudinal shift most was the development of the Whitehead torpedo and
the periscope. The Whitehead torpedo was a fairly reliable, self-propelled
underwater projectile with the capability of sinking enemy vessels at great
distances. Originally launched from surface torpedo boats and destroyers,
the torpedo was considered by many to be more effective when fired from
a submarine. Advocates of the submarine pointed out that this kind of
craft had two advantages over surface vessels for the delivery of this
weapon. First, owing to its ability for diving, a lone submarine could fire

its torpedoes into a fleet or convoy during daylight as well as darkness. Second, its underwater milieu made it less vulnerable to attack once it had released its torpedoes.[2] Prior to the invention of the periscope, submarines were essentially running blind while underwater, the operator having to bring the viewing ports in the conning tower above the surface to establish his course and align the craft for firing torpedoes. This maneuver would, of course, expose the submarine's position to enemy vessels. John Holland had experimented with a camera lucida, a lens and mirror system mounted in a long tube that projected an image onto a white sheet of paper. This arrangement did not provide the observer with any idea of distance as it was essentially the same as viewing a photograph. Simon Lake undertook a solution to the submarine's blindness by inventing the omniscope (first called the "skalomniscope"), which was the forerunner of the modern periscope. The omniscope was a series of lenses and prisms that not only provided a view of the entire horizon from within the submarine but also permitted an estimate of range. Somewhat later, Sir Howard Grubb, of England, constructed a similar device that was to become standard in submarines of the day. The David now had "eyes" that would enhance its concealment.[3]

One of the first to advocate the use of the submarine as an adjunct to a naval fleet was British admiral Sir John Fisher. As early as 1904 he had stated, "I don't think it is even faintly realized—the immense impending revolution which the submarines will effect as offensive weapons of war." He would from that point on refer to them as "the battleships of the future."[4] Fisher, it might be recalled, was the man responsible for initiating the construction of the dreadnoughts that formed the backbone of the British fleet. A man of considerable foresight, he did not take long to realize the vulnerability of these bastions of the seas to the smaller, underwater marauders. Britain had begun construction of submarines in 1900 in the face of considerable opposition from many naval officers. Admiral Charles Beresford once remarked, "The submarine is always in a fog. They [are] merely a defensive weapon, and therefore unsuitable for use in an offensive fleet like the British."[5]

As mentioned earlier, Isaac Rice of the Electric Boat Company had established a contractual agreement with the British firm of Vickers-Maxim & Sons (later Vickers Ltd.) to construct submarines for the British Navy. This agreement had run a contorted route through Rice's connections with the Rothschild banking house during April of 1900. Under Fisher's direction, Vickers began constructing submarines in earnest. Vickers also began purchasing the company's stock to ease a financial crunch that

Electric Boat was suffering. By 1903, Rice and Vickers held the majority of stock in this American company, a situation that did not sit well with many members of Congress.

In 1911, another important player in the submarine saga of the First World War came onto the scene, Britain's First Lord of the Admiralty, Winston Leonard Spencer Churchill. Although initially ambivalent toward submarines, Churchill's attitude would change significantly and he would, under Fisher's tutelage, become a staunch supporter of submarines over the dreadnought. The two men would play important roles in the outcome of the war that was brewing and advance the importance of submarines in the world's navies.[6] At the outbreak of war in 1914, the British Navy had 73 submarines of various vintages. These included the "A" and "B" classes, which had been built by Electric Boat and modeled after the original *Holland*. They were considered suitable only for harbor defense. The larger "C", "D", and "E" classes were capable of operating in the open sea for a few days and were utilized for the defense of the Firth of Forth, the mouth of the Thames, the Strait of Dover, and the Heligoland Bight.[7]

Across the Channel, Germany had begun to challenge Britain's rule of the sea. By the turn of the century, the German economy had outstripped that of the British Empire, and Imperial Germany was now poised to become a maritime rival. The naval challenge that developed can be linked to the activities of one man, Admiral Alfred von Tirpitz. Tirpitz was a torpedo officer who rose to the rank of admiral, eventually becoming the secretary of the Imperial Naval Office (Reichsmarineamt) in 1897. This administrative office was responsible for formulating and directing naval building programs. In his planning, Tirpitz considered Britain to be Germany's most dangerous opponent and recommended a program to build the greatest number of battleships possible.[8] During his early tenure as secretary, Tirpitz appeared to show little interest in the construction of submarines. When asked in 1902 why Germany was not constructing submarines, he replied, "We can't afford it. We can afford the money, but not the brains. We think we can utilize our mental energy to better advantage in developing fighting ships for the supremacy of the sea."[9] This thinking would be altered significantly within a few short years. By 1907, Germany was spending nine million marks a year on submarine construction. At the outset of the war, Germany had only twenty-eight submarines, eighteen of which were fit only for coastal defense. The submarines designated U-19 (the "U" signifying "Untersee Bote") through U-28 were seagoing craft whose capabilities had not yet been fully exploited by the German Navy.[10] Production and use of the German submarines would increase. It would be Tirpitz's unrestricted use of the U-boats that would ultimately draw the United States into the First World War.

Governments are notoriously slow-moving entities. By 1914, Fisher, who had left the Admirality in 1910, was becoming frustrated with the lack of response to his pleas for increased submarine construction. In letters to the controller of the navy and the prime minister, Fisher referred to Britain's submarine construction as "the most serious thing at present affecting the British Empire.... We had more submarines 4 years ago when I left the admiralty than we have now . . . and the Germans then nil. Now they have more high sea submarines than ourselves. . . . I have said all this to Winston till I am sick! (and made him sick too I fear!). Myself I should drop a Dreadnought secretly & go in for 20 submarines instead."[11]

As August, 1914, approached, Canada now became entwined in the Gordian knot surrounding submarine construction. Fearing that Britain would shortly go to war with Germany and that this would open Canada to attack, Sir Richard McBride, Premier of British Columbia, purchased two submarines from Electric Boat. The submarines had been built in California for the Chilean government, but when a controversy developed over specifications, a door was opened for the Canadian purchase. These would become the first submarines of the Canadian Navy. The craft were purchased with uncharacteristic governmental speed, and they quickly left American waters on August 5, 1914. The following day, a U.S. Navy cruiser was sent to retrieve the submarines, but it was too late. Contraband of war had been sold in violation of U.S. neutrality laws.[12]

The events occurring between 1905 and 1917 were to significantly affect both the Lake Torpedo Boat Company and the Electric Boat Company, bringing into question the neutrality of the United States as a world power. The clandestine events involving Britain, Canada, and the United States' largest steel manufacturer, Bethlehem Steel, would become a quagmire of political intrigue.

Charles Schwab is recognized as one of America's leading industrialists, and one who, during the first decade of the nineteenth century, rapidly rose to become one of the leaders within the Andrew Carnegie industrial empire. In 1904 his prominence permitted him to organize and build one of the country's steel giants, the Bethlehem Steel Corporation. Although heavily involved with the production of commercial steel for buildings and bridges, Schwab generated most of the company's profits through the production of armaments. So it was not unexpected that he would eventually become linked with Electric Boat in the construction of submarines. Schwab's travels in Europe just prior to the world war resulted in talks with British officials concerning the possibilities of building and delivering the implements of war to England. Based upon previous shipments of uncompleted war materials (as had been done by Simon Lake and the Electric Boat Company), Schwab assured the British that he could supply the needed implements of war. However, Schwab now faced an increasing concern by members of the U.S. government over the violation of neutrality laws. Ironically, this movement to halt illegal arms shipments stemmed from a neutrality violation that occurred between the United States and England during the American Civil War.[13] In July of 1862, the Confederacy had purchased a warship from Britain that was armed in the Azores and subsequently named the *Alabama*. This ship was to wreak havoc on Union shipping during the war and generate outcries from the United States regarding the sale of contraband to a belligerent. It was not until 1871 that the matter was finally resolved when the U.S. and England, under the terms of the Treaty of Washington, agreed that a neutral government was required to operate with "due diligence" when dealing with a belligerent government. The outcome of the Geneva Tribunal in 1872 was that England paid the United States $15.5 million for the losses suffered.[14] Now, in 1914, the tables had turned and it was warring England vying for contraband from the "neutral" United States.

Schwab seemed to know that he was in for a fight and argued that the materials he intended to send to England fell into the category of ordinary contraband, citing the events of the Russo-Japanese War. What followed became a tangled web of legal hassling and bureaucratic verbiage. Schwab wanted to deliver submarines to Britain, who direly needed these undersea boats. The initial outcome of decisions in Washington regarding the shipment of contraband was that it could be accomplished in one of two ways. First, finished hulls that lacked armament could be shipped to a belligerent country, where they would be completed. The second option was to ship the hulls piecemeal for assembly and finishing in the country of destination. This was exactly what Schwab was waiting for, and he immediately ordered Electric Boat and Bethlehem Steel to begin construction of twenty submarines.[15]

Schwab's plants were now beehives of activity. But another obstacle loomed in his path: President Woodrow Wilson. Under the influence of Secretary of State William Jennings Bryan, Wilson rescinded the previous interpretation of the neutrality laws, which, for the moment, put an end to any submarines being shipped to Britain. A man of lesser determination would have been devastated, but Schwab considered this just another challenge. He would circumvent the president's dictates. The plan was relatively simple: Vickers would establish a plant in Canada, and Bethlehem Steel would supply materials and components to the Canadian plant for completion into submarines for Britain. Electric Boat Company employees would supervise the construction, and their company would receive compensation for their services. Although publicly denying the construction of submarines for Britain in the press, Schwab had succeeded in accomplishing his goal of supplying the British with their needed implements of war.[16]

Besides the financial gain for Bethlehem Steel, Schwab's activities had other benefits. The fledgling submarine industry of the United States, as represented by the Electric Boat Company and, later, the Lake Torpedo Boat Company, would be strengthened. Electric Boat gained immediate financial support from contracts through Vickers, not only in England, but now also in Canada.

On June 28, 1914, the spark that was to ignite World War I was struck. Archduke Francis Ferdinand, heir to the Austrian throne, and his wife were assassinated in Sarajevo, Yugoslavia (formerly Austria-Hungary). The war that Fisher (in 1910) had predicted would break out in the autumn of 1914 had come, and, although the events in Sarajevo precipitated the conflict, much of the real impetus for war lay in the wake of Germany's preparations for naval expansion, which was the root of British hostility.[17]

Great Britain declared war on Germany on August 4, 1914. The German General Staff had planned a quick defeat of France while holding the Russians at bay on the Eastern Front. The Western Front, however, quickly degenerated into the stalemate of trench warfare. The Germans threw everything they had against the Western Front, hoping to defeat the English and French before the Americans entered the fray. At sea, the Germans were also faring poorly. The Battle of Jutland, which occurred in May of 1916, although tactically not a defeat for the Germans, demonstrated the superiority of the British fleet, particularly in blockading both Germany's warships and commercial vessels to the point of the country becoming a beleaguered garrison. But the close blockading tactics used in previous engagements by the British required modification because of the advances made with mines, torpedoes, airships, and submarines, as the Russo-Japanese War had demonstrated.[18] The submarine provided ample reason for the change in tactics when, on September 5, 1914, the German U-boat U-21 sent the HMS *Pathfinder* to the bottom in the Fifth of Forth. Three weeks later, on September 22, U-9 sank the three British cruisers *Aboukir*, *Cressy*, and *Houge* in a single afternoon. The sinkings resulted in the loss of 36,000 tons and the lives of 1,370. The efficacy of using submarines as

offensive weapons had become apparent. Germany increased its submarine production to include not only large, diesel-powered, seagoing craft
(from U-19 onward) but also seventeen smaller submarines (UB 1–17, with
a 127-ton surface displacement) for harbor defense. Additionally, fifteen
intermediate-sized minelayers (UC 1–15) were built.[19] The British response
was to increase the production of submarines. Three weeks after the sinking of the three British cruisers, Churchill not only increased orders for
submarine construction but also requested designs for faster, fleet submarines. From a design standpoint, the British had to resort to steam power
to achieve the speeds Churchill sought. The craft were designated the K-
class, capable of surface speeds of twenty-four knots. This speed was sufficient to keep up with the battle fleet and then permit them to serve as
the fleet's advanced scouting line.[20]

Why the German High Command had not begun to build oceangoing
submarines prior to August of 1914 undoubtedly stemmed from the lack
of reliance most German naval authorities placed on the offensive value
of these undersea boats. However, there are two additional possibilities:
(1) The Germans had planned for a quick victory, estimated to be late in
1914 or early 1915, and submarines ordered at the start of the war would
not have been completed until 1917; and (2) Germany had only one facility
to produce submarines in 1914 (Krupp). To build submarines, Germany
first would have needed to build additional shipyards at which to construct and launch these craft.[21]

In February of 1915, the success of the British blockade forced Tirpitz
to give the order for unrestricted submarine warfare to commence. The
waters around the British Isles were declared a war zone, and all enemy
warships and vessels of commerce were considered fair game. Germany
was attempting to wear down the British fleet to the point of equality with
the German fleet (the so-called "equalizing campaign") and to cut Britain's supply lines, a tactic it believed would permit Germany to win the
war in six months. The tactic was doomed to failure, and in the end the
German fleet was relegated to supporting its U-boats. Unrestricted submarine warfare proved as devastating for the British as it did the Germans.[22] Under U.S. pressure, the Germans agreed to certain concessions.
Neutral vessels and hospital and relief ships were exempted, and the U-
boats were required to investigate the nationality of any ship before an
attack was to be made. However, by the following autumn, unrestricted
submarine warfare was again reinstituted. The results were disastrous. On
May 7, 1915, the German U-20 torpedoed the *Lusitania,* an event that

clearly altered the desire for neutrality in the United States. Of the 1,198 noncombatants killed in the attack, 94 were children and infants and 128 were Americans. The submarine had created a schism between the two countries.[23] Simon Lake had predicted this sinking more than a year before it happened. In fact, recognizing the serious threat that the German submarines posed, he had spent several thousand dollars in newspaper advertising warning Americans not to sail on the *Lusitania.*[24]

The following year witnessed a series of events that drew the United States closer to a state of war with Germany. Besides the sinking of Allied shipping, an instructor of German at Cornell University, Eric Munther, planted a bomb that destroyed the U.S. Senate reception room on July 2, 1916. The following day, he attempted to assassinate J. P. Morgan, Jr., and then committed suicide on July 6, 1916. These events were followed by bombings of ammunition storage areas and at least one bridge. The spectacular destruction of the munitions arsenal on Black Tom Island, New Jersey, was an act of sabotage that cost the country $22 million.[25] By April of 1917, the United States was ready to declare war on Germany.

The saber rattling in Europe during the early 1900s had a significant effect upon U.S. naval authorities. The navy's concern with having the most modern submarines, coupled with Congress's investigation of the Electric Boat monopoly on submarine construction, had caused a door that had previously been closed to Simon Lake to suddenly become ajar. In 1908, through the efforts of numerous individuals, particularly Fred B. Whitney, chairman of the board of the Lake Torpedo Boat Company, the company was to build its first submarine for the U.S. Navy. The agreement called for Lake to build the craft at his company's expense. She would be purchased if and when her performance met the navy's requirements. This arrangement was in stark contrast to that provided Electric Boat, which had received immediate payment upon signing a contract. It was a gamble, but it was still a banner day for Lake and his company. They would begin the construction of the *Seal,* their first American military submarine.

Her keel was laid on February 2, 1909, at the Newport News Shipbuilding Company in Newport News, Virginia. She was 161 feet in length and was the first navy submarine ever equipped with Lake's characteristic wheels. Her estimated price was $450,000. In addition to the standard bow torpedo tubes, Lake added a novel series of revolving deck torpedo tubes to increase her firepower. The *Seal* was also equipped with Lake's patented diving chamber, included so she could also perform mine-laying duties.

fig. 20. The SS *19 1/2*, Simon Lake's *Seal*–the only craft in the U.S. Navy to ever bear a 1/2 designation. From Lake Torpedo Boat Company, *The Development of the Lake Type Submarine* (Bridgeport, Conn.: Lake Torpedo Boat Company, 1910)

Additionally, the diving chamber served as an escape hatch should the craft encounter difficulties. She was launched on February 9, 1911, sponsored by Miss Margaret V. Lake, daughter of the inventor.[26]

During her trials, the *Seal* exceeded all of the requirements set forth by the navy. Her contracted surface speed was 14 knots, but she made 14.7 knots; the contracted submerged speed of 9 1/2 knots was exceeded by 1 1/2 knots. The *Seal* was capable of traveling over 4,000 miles on the surface at 8 knots and 2,500 miles in a semisubmerged condition. The value of even-keel diving in controlling the submarine was demonstrated by her ability to hold her depth within two feet when traveling at 11 knots and within one foot at a speed of 9 1/2 knots. Depth testing of a new submarine was usually accomplished by lowering the empty craft to various test depths from a marine derrick. The *Seal*'s depth test, however, was undertaken with a full crew with Captain Sloan Danehower in command. She dove to 256 feet, a record dive for submarines of the day. To demonstrate that the diver's chamber would allow crew members to exit the submarine in an emergency, Danehower dove out of the chamber and swam to the surface during a shallow diving exercise.[27] His exhibition impressed navy officials watching the demonstration, as many still held reservations about the safety of underwater craft.

Simon Lake was proud of the Seal and her performance, but there is more to this story. It appears that old animosities die hard. As mentioned earlier, unlike the Electric Boat Company, which upon receiving a naval contract to build a submarine automatically began receiving funds for the construction, the Lake Torpedo Boat Company was forced to build the *Seal* from its own funds and did not receive any compensation until after the boat's trials and final acceptance by the navy. Electric Boat officials were aware of the financial difficulties Lake's company was suffering at the time. Although their allegation is unproven, many Lake Torpedo Boat officers believed that the navy's requirement that Lake's company build the *Seal* at its own expense may have been another ploy by Electric Boat to maintain its monopoly on submarines.

One further incident points out a petty indignity that Lake was subjected to during the construction of the *Seal*. Apparently, the Lake submarine had been given the hull number SS-19 by the navy. Naval officials then realized that two other submarines under construction had been given the numbers 19 and 20. To correct the situation, the navy renumbered the *Seal*, making it SS-19 1/2, the only submarine in the history of the fleet to bear a "1/2" designation. Lake took this apparent jab in a good-hearted manner, laughing at the fact that he had provided the government with half a submarine whose performance outdistanced anything that the navy had at the time. Six years later, in December of 1917, the SS-20 sank and the navy corrected this situation by redesignating the *Seal* the SS-20.[28]

The government contract with the Lake Torpedo Boat Company signaled the breaking of Electric Boat's monopoly and the U.S. Navy's acceptance of the Lake type of submarine. Governmental orders for additional submarines were now placed with the Lake Torpedo Boat Company, and the plant on Seaview Avenue in Bridgeport, Connecticut, was expanded to handle the additional business. By 1916, a second, adjoining shipyard covering almost two thirds of a mile was opened, and the plant was employing more than five thousand people. The coastline bristled with the pilings that made up the ways from which submarines were launched. The company also licensed the California Shipbuilding Yard to build submarines on the West Coast for the Pacific Fleet.[29]

Between 1911 and 1922, the Lake Torpedo Boat Company would produce thirty-three submarines for the U.S. government, each costing approximately a half million dollars (see Appendix A). Many of these craft would see action during the world war and also serve as trainers for America's developing submarine force. One of these boats, the S-48, is of particular note. She was completed in 1922 and was still part of the fleet in 1930

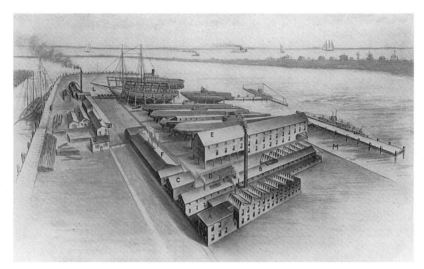

fig. 21. Artist's rendering of the Lake Torpedo Boat Company in Bridgeport, Connecticut. From Lake Torpedo Boat Company, *The Development of the Lake Type Submarine* (Bridgeport, Conn.: Lake Torpedo Boat Company, 1910)

when a thirty-year-old officer was assigned to her for duty. His name was Hyman Rickover, the man who would become Admiral Rickover and take on the responsibility for the design and production of the power plant for the *Nautilus*, the world's first atomic submarine.[30]

Although Simon Lake's fortunes were changing for the better during this period, the same cannot be said for those of his major competitor, John Holland. Removed as president of the company he founded when it was incorporated into the Electric Boat Company, he would build no more submarines. The discouragement of the man can be seen in a letter he wrote in 1909:

> Uncle Sam's officials turned their back on me because I criticized alleged improvements made on the Holland. I did not graduate from Annapolis. I am not disloyal or without patriotism, but I am ashamed of the boasted efficiency of our bureaus of construction. Nations got a terrible sample of poor submarine construction when the A-8 went to the bottom in English waters. I charged the English Admiralty with careless construction, and our Admiral Capps charged me with indiscretion. When I review the supposed improvements in submarine work by our youthful naval architects, graduates of Annapolis, I am se-

verely arraigned by these selfsame youngsters. They presume to know more about submarines than I do. They favor nothing but what comes from England. Uncle Sam will have nothing to do with me, and I am sure I have little respect for English naval constructors as they have for me.[31]

John Holland died on August 12, 1914, in Newark, New Jersey, at the age of seventy-three, three weeks before the outbreak of hostilities that would emphasize the potential of the submarine as an offensive weapon of naval warfare. He did not live to bear witness to the devastation these underwater craft could inflict upon the world's navies.[32]

Simon Lake's contribution to the German war effort is witnessed in another of his inventions, the cargo-carrying submarine. By 1915, the blockade by the Royal Navy had effectively sealed off Germany from the rest of the world. German naval authorities under Admiral von Tirpitz were advocating increased submarine production and the waging of unrestricted submarine warfare as a means of crippling the British Fleet. The civilian government, led by Reich Chancellor Theobald Bethmann-Hollweg, was attempting to find a way to run the blockade. The answer appeared to lie in the building of cargo U-boats, large transport submarines capable of carrying large quantities of needed war materials.[33]

Although the Germans would credit a Krupp engineer and designer named Rudolf Erbach for originating the cargo U-boat concept in 1914, Simon Lake had actually proposed the concept and provided drawings to Krupp some five years prior. The basic idea behind the cargo carrier was simple. If a craft could not successfully run around or through a blockade, then it would run *under* it. Like all of her military sister craft, the proposed cargo carrier was to be of double-hulled construction, still another concept introduced by Simon Lake. Construction began in 1915 on two cargo-carrying submarines, the *Deutschland* and *Bremen,* ostensibly by a civilian organization called the Deutsche Ozean Reederei. The *Deutschland* was built first and was, by 1916 standards, a large submarine (213 feet long with a 29.2-foot beam), estimated to carry about half the cargo of a small freighter (six hundred tons). She was launched on March 28, 1916, and made her first crossing of the Atlantic between June 23 and July 8, 1916, under the command of Captain Lebrecht Köenig. She would carry a small fortune in dyestuffs and pharmaceuticals to the United States. It was hoped that she would return with a cargo of needed supplies.[34]

Civilian members of the German company fronting the construction of the *Deutschland* had purchased waterfront property in Baltimore under the name of the Eastern Forwarding Company. They also leased the State Pier in New London, Connecticut. The idea was to establish civilian status for the two submarines since legitimate commercial craft were given a longer period of grace at dockside to load and unload cargo. By law, ships of belligerent nations could remain no longer than twenty-four hours, after which they could be interned for the duration of the war.[35] The *Deutschland* arrived at Baltimore on July 8, 1916, and one of the first to greet Captain Köenig was Simon Lake. When Lake had learned that the German submarine was sailing for the United States, he immediately contacted his lawyers to determine whether he could bring suit against the German government for patent infringements. The British, who had been carefully following the voyage of the *Deutschland,* were elated at the prospects of seeing the submarine attached. Lake's comment on the situation strengthened the British hopes.[36] He stated, "It is entirely possible for a German submarine to cross the Atlantic. But if one does enter an American port it will be met by a process server. The crew will be surprised at the reception, no doubt, but in America the Lake Torpedo Boat Company controls the rights to make and use my devices."[37]

Lake and Fred Whitney were greeted warmly by Captain Köenig and an agent for the North German Line named Paul Hilken, and then invited on board for a tour of the submarine. After the tour, Lake let the Germans know the purpose of his visit, stating that he had "another purpose in coming to see you. I know the *Deutschland* has been built in evasion of my patents. If I can prove this is so I propose to attach her."[38] Hilken, in a dazed and shocked condition, replied, "You wouldn't do that. She's your baby."[39] As the conversation continued, Lake was to learn that Germany had indeed stolen his designs. Further, it was made clear to him that the *Deutschland* was being used as a blockade runner to deliver commercial goods, such as aniline dyes, on which Germany held a monopoly (the *Deutschland*'s cargo was worth an estimated $6 million) and return with supplies for the German people. The last portion of the statement was a lie, since the *Deutschland*'s return cargo consisted of four hundred tons of nickel, ninety tons of tin, four hundred tons of crude rubber, and a half-ton of jute—supplies obviously for the benefit of the war effort.[40]

Lake had been fooled. Captain Köenig, noted for his charm, apparently convinced Lake that his cargo carrier would be returning to Germany with supplies for the German people. Taken in, Lake's response angered the British: "If the *Deutschland* were a warship I'd darn well try to do something. But my sympathies are with the women and children who are made to suffer by reason of the blockade England is carrying on."[41] In an attempt to sweeten the ploy and further divert Lake from thoughts of attaching the *Deutschland*, Köenig discussed with Lake the possibility of his building a fleet of cargo-carrying submarines for Germany. Two days later, Lake held a press conference to announce that he and Krupp would form a company to build cargo-carrying submarines in the United States for Germany. Lake seemed to be returning to his roots, demonstrating the commercial applicability of submarines. However, the plan never reached fruition.

The *Deutschland* would make a second voyage to the United States, a trip requiring twenty-two days (October 8 to November 1, 1916). Later, she was converted to a military submarine and managed to sink ten steamers. She was surrendered to the Royal Navy at Harwich on November 24, 1918. In December of that year, she was put on display in London as a trophy of war, and three years later she was sold for scrap worth two hundred pounds.[42] Her sister ship, *Bremen*, suffered a different fate. On her maiden voyage to the United States, she was lost with all hands. Nothing is known about the cause of her loss.[43]

The signing of the armistice with Germany on November 11, 1918, and the Treaty of Versailles in 1919 ended World War I and signaled the onset of a short-lived period of peace in the world. These signings also heralded the beginning of the end for the Lake Torpedo Boat Company. Between 1910 and 1918, the company had grown into a complex worth more than $2 million. It was the only plant of its kind, specializing in the construction of submarines. But the world was tired of war, and many naively held "the belief that the possession of large armaments was by itself a cause of war; and that if only the nations would disarm, . . . peace would be assured."[44] Disarmament, however, was not a simple matter, and negotiations regarding arms limitation always seemed to take place in an atmosphere of constant rivalry. This was especially true for the talks between the principal naval powers. The discussions caused a revival of the long-standing antagonism between France and Britain. Similarly, the United States and Britain expressed grave concern about Japan as a rising naval power. France and Italy were never able to resolve their rivalry. However, the conflict that was to influence the negotiations the most was the one that existed between the United States and Britain, the so-called Anglo-American antagonism. It stemmed from the U.S. challenge to Britain's long-standing maritime and commercial superiority.[45] In many respects, Britain was now in a position with the United States that resembled her position with Germany in the years preceding the war, especially after the financial drain placed upon her economy by the war. The American viewpoint was that Britain would "strive to maintain naval supremacy for the defense of the empire . . . and for the domination of world markets."[46]

The naval clauses in the Treaty of Versailles initiated the first round of disagreement between the Americans and the British regarding disarmament.[47] As might be expected, submarines were a major stumbling point. After experiencing unrestricted submarine warfare, the predominant feeling of the British was to abolish submarines, a view also expressed by many pacifists in America. Simon Lake was beginning to see the writing on the wall. He stated:

> England lives on its ocean freight-carrying business. If England could abolish the submarine and continue to hold the seas with her fleet of battleships and cruisers her position as Mistress of the Seas would continue to be unassailable. The English need clicked with the glary-eyed idealism of the Americans. We were tired of war, sick of the sounds of the words, weary of the smell of blood, disgusted with greed and barbarism of both sides, and anxious to get back to the pleasant shades of sentiment and the unrealistic talk of brotherly love and universal democracy.[48]

The Washington Conference of 1921–22 brought together civilian delegates from Britain, Japan, France, Italy, and the United States (China, Holland, Portugal, and Belgium were also invited, but their input was restricted to discussions related to their territorial and economic interests in the Pacific and Far East). Soviet Russia was excluded from the conference.[49] The main objective of the conference was to discuss Pacific and Far Eastern affairs, with an emphasis on naval limitation.[50] The British Empire Delegation was led by Lord Arthur James Balfour. He let it be known that the intention of the British delegation was to protect and safeguard the vital interests of the British Empire, stating: "From the discussions which took place at the Cabinet before my departure I formed the clear impression that the ultimate aim of the British Empire Delegation . . . is to secure the largest possible limitation of armaments consistent with the safety of the British Empire."[51] At the conference, Balfour would reiterate his nation's desire for the total abolition of submarines. Although the U.S. and French contingents opposed total abolition, the former was working under the constraints of President Warren Harding, who was publicly committed to an all-round reduction in armaments.[52]

The conference was to produce nine treaties and adopt twelve resolutions regarding naval limitations. Besides placing constraints on the tonnages of vessels each nation was entitled to maintain, Senator Elihu Root of the American delegation introduced a resolution requiring submarines to operate under the "visit and search" rule before seizure of any merchant ships. Although the conference failed to place any restrictions on the number of submarines any nation could build, the treaties imposed drastic limitations on naval construction by the world's naval powers. The Root Resolutions essentially reduced the effectiveness of the submarine.[53]

Simon Lake's response to the Washington Treaty was predictable. He sent a letter to the meeting's delegates expressing his concern about their recommendations. He wrote:

> I agree with you that the *offensive* type of submarine should be abolished. It is hard for naval experts to adopt the policy of "let well enough alone." They are always reaching out for something better, especially as to increasing speeds, radius of action and increased armament. In a race for naval supremacy this is an essential, but if the policy of providing a navy for *defense* only is adopted by the Conference, then the requirement of defense only need be considered. . . . As a student of the possibilities of the use of the submarine both in commercial and in the military field, for a period of over thirty years, I have come to the conclusion that it offers not only the cheapest and best means of defense that any county can provide for its protection but that it has also the capability of being developed for constructive purposes instead of destructive uses as in the military submarine. I believe this craft will be the most important adjunct introduced into the shipping world since the advent of steam propulsion, and England is the last country that should put a ban on its development because it is likely to become of more importance to her than any other nation.[54]

The delegates who received this letter replied sympathetically to Lake. Lord Balfour did not bother to answer.

One effect of the treaty in the United States was a reduction in submarine construction, an effect Simon Lake would, for the remainder of his days, blame on Lord Balfour. Considering the situation in hindsight, Lake would comment in his autobiography that "[i]t was the most complete triumph of romance over the harder facts of life I have ever known. . . . We completely forgot that we were planning all these good things for the human race, which has not changed materially within the range of recorded history. The American thought was to do a sweet thing on a great scale. The English idea was to get rid of the submarine."[55]

By 1922, submarine construction at the Lake Torpedo Boat Company had come to a complete standstill. It was costing Lake about fifty thousand dollars a year to maintain an inactive plant. When he and his board members finally realized that there would be no further submarine contracts, Lake closed the doors. The plant was sold, bringing only about 5 percent of its cost or replacement value. During the war, Lake had also opened the Housatonic Shipbuilding Company in Stratford, Connecticut, where he built wooden ships for the U.S. Army. The Washington Treaty also succeeded in putting an end to this endeavor.[56] During the war, Lake had rejected contracts for foreign submarines, patriotically concentrating his efforts on American submarine construction. It was an activity that came back to haunt him when he no longer had a market for his submarines in Europe. His main competitor, the Electric Boat Company, had continued to seek foreign contracts and to build submarines for various foreign governments, an activity that permitted Electric Boat Company to survive the years of idealism.[57]

Saddened but undaunted, Lake turned his interests to other endeavors. The loss of his company was disheartening for him, but it did not slow the intrepid inventor for long. Robert Blezard put it best when he wrote: "For the ruddy-faced inventor and entrepreneur, who bore a resemblance in spirit as well as looks to Teddy Roosevelt, the demise of the Lake Torpedo Boat Company did not become a personal tragedy which might have scarred a weaker man for life."[58]

Simon Lake put this phase of his life into perspective during an interview in 1932, an interview that provides a good deal of insight into Simon Lake the man.

> Having had Puritan and Shaker ancestors, I am a Pacifist at heart myself, but having spent some years in foreign countries, living for a time in Russia, Austria, Germany and England, I have become convinced that the millennium has not yet arrived. . . . And, so, much to my regret, I have seen the error of my early pacifist theories gradually disappear, because human nature seems to be working much the same as has worked since men first fought with their naked hands with the wild beasts for their food, and puny man has only succeeded in outliving the monster animals that he had to compete against because of his greater intelligence which enabled him to devise weapons and habitations that gave him protection.
>
> I cannot believe that Mr. Wilson's idealistic theory of put-

ting the whole world into a common "melting pot" and that we will all come out pure gold, will be realized for many centuries to come, and think the only safe way for us to do, if we wish to retain the rights fought for by our ancestors is to do as Theodore Roosevelt said, "Speak gently, and carry a big stick."[59]

Lake would now turn his inventive genius toward an endeavor unrelated to submarines: the first attempt at precasting pipe and entire houses from concrete.

CHAPTER 8

Sunshine Homes and Concrete Pipes

That they are not a pipe for fortune's finger ...
—William Shakespeare, Hamlet, Act III

L ike many inventors, Simon Lake was not a specialist but a generalist. His active and innovative mind was quick to identify a problem, and then even quicker to seek and provide solutions. He did not limit himself to submarines and underwater technologies. Around 1916, he observed a need for housing in and around the larger industrial areas that were becoming involved in the war effort. He also recognized that this need would increase after the war when the veterans returned from the conflict raging in Europe. As a result, he formed the Lakeolith Corporation, a company whose specialty was the construction of inexpensive, prefabricated housing for the common laborer.

By 1925, with time on his hands due to the closure of the Lake Torpedo Boat Company, Lake began working in earnest on his prefabricated homes from the Lake Engineering Company plant in Stratford, Connecticut. The company operated under the name of Sunshine Homes. Lake's patented process permitted him to preform reinforced, double-insulated concrete walls, floors, and roofs up to twelve feet in width by thirty feet in length. Doors and window frames were cast in place at the factory. Lake had succeeded in duplicating the production line concept of Henry Ford for the mass production of houses.[1] In addressing America's housing shortage,

Lake said, "I came to the conclusion that the only way in which this important question could be solved was to abandon the old-fashion way of putting a house together, piece by piece, on the spot, and assemble its parts on the Ford plan."[2]

The wall structures had undergone stringent building code tests at the Columbia University Laboratories under the scrutiny of New York City's engineers. They were found to be more than suitable as a replacement for standard construction materials typically put together in a time-consuming, piecemeal fashion. Lake estimated that a single home could be constructed for $500 per room, excluding heating, plumbing, and foundation. Using the same technology for apartment buildings, he estimated that they could be built for $350 per room.[3] The need for housing, coupled with the prices Lake was quoting for their construction, stirred a great deal of interest for a number of companies. For example, he was approached by Joseph Fells, president of the famed soap manufacturing company, about the possibility of using the Lakeolith technology to construct a whole village for workers in England. Fells was a philanthropist who had already provided a large housing complex for workers. Lake pointed out to him that such complexes, in order to maintain the contentedness of its inhabitants, should be cheap, comfortable, permanent, aesthetically pleasing, and convenient in every way.[4] Unfortunately, World War II intervened, and nothing ever came of Lake's plans for better housing. Igor Sikorsky, inventor of the helicopter, had formed the Sikorsky Aeroplane Company in Bridgeport, Connecticut. Like Fells, Sikorsky was concerned with housing for his employees. In a personal letter, Lake mentions the possibility of constructing two hundred houses for the fledgling helicopter company. However, this project never became a reality, either. The Sears and Roebuck Company and the American Tobacco Company also expressed an initial interest in Lakeolith. During the early stages of President Roosevelt's New Deal, Lake offered the technology to the government, but in all three cases, the parties declined to accept any contracts.[5]

Lake did construct several buildings in Connecticut and New York. In viewing photographs of these structures today, one is struck by their architectural cleanness. It is difficult to understand why this technology was not accepted at the time, but there are at least two possible reasons for the nonacceptance of Lakeolith. First, there tends to be a general skepticism surrounding any new technology in all fields of endeavor. Henry Ford was considered a heretic when he set out to provide an automobile for the common man in the days when the horse was king. The idea of manned flight and subsequent air passenger service were the "pipe dreams" of two brothers at Kitty Hawk. A lack of imagination and foresight is all too common in the world. The idea of a prefabricated house in 1916 was new, and no matter how Lake tried, he could not overcome the refractory attitudes toward prebuilt housing. A second reason for his difficulties may have been Lake's own doing. In his advertising for Lakeolith, he continually pointed out that the housing shortage was, in large part, due to the limited amount of skilled labor available for construction. By maintaining a small labor force, individuals within the force could ask for and receive unprecedented wages. His Lakeolith process required laborers with minimal training, thereby replacing the higher-paid bricklayer and plasterer. This form of advertising served to alienate the labor unions of the time and create an adversarial atmosphere. Years later, when asked why the Lakeolith process was not accepted at the time, Lake attributed his failed business to what he called "skrimshanking bellyachers," his term for unionized construction workers. In his autobiography, Lake reasoned:

> The obstacle that I met at the outset was the fear on the part of organized labor that the building trade unions would lose work if prefabricated houses were erected on any large scale. I believe that this is a false assumption. That a few men would suffer is true, but the advantage to the labor body as a whole seems to me to be very great. I have convinced a few labor leaders of this, but others have not been able to recognize that, for every man laid off in one particular trade, many more jobs would be available for other tradesmen, and labor as a whole would benefit because of the cheaper and better housing which would be provided.[6]

Lake was not one to give up on an idea he considered valid. Through the years he would continue to return to his concrete experimentation and attempt to apply it to other areas. Shortly before the outbreak of World War II, he wrote President Roosevelt suggesting a pipeline made from preformed concrete pipes be used to deliver oil from the Southwest to the refineries on the East Coast, thereby eliminating the oil tankers which he recognized early on to be susceptible to sinking by German submarines—an event that, in fact, did occur off the Atlantic Coast and in the Gulf of Mexico. In essence, he predated the Alaskan Pipeline by at least three decades. As with many of the schemes he was to relay to the president, he was thanked for his concern and innovativeness, but little came for his efforts.[7]

Simon Lake was a man whose untiring mind would nor permit him to remain inactive nor devoted to a single endeavor for any length of time. He seemed always to be up to any challenge that required the development of some device to accomplish a particular objective. In a discussion with Herbert Hoover at the Engineers' Club in New York, Hoover expressed a need for a dredging machine that would permit him to extract small quantities of gold from bottom sands. He claimed that there was a fortune to be made in the Lena Delta in Russia, where the sands held $250 of gold per yard (when gold was worth $36 an ounce). The discussion piqued Lake's inventiveness and set him off developing a screening device to extract gold from bottom sands. Within a few months, he had a device that worked. He salted a sand sample with fifty pieces of gold ranging in size from flakes to nuggets. In most trials, all fifty pieces of gold were retrieved after a single pass through the machine, always collected after a second pass. His thoughts immediately turned to the gold-bearing soils of Alaska. But then his wide-ranging interests set him off gadfly fashion on yet another project: he decided to build a second salvage tube with which to re-enter the salvaging business.[8] This decision may have been prompted by a letter he received from a Lt. Col. Foss in England regarding the status of the salvage tube Lake had constructed for his attempt to salvage the *Lutine* treasure, which had been halted by the outbreak of war.[9] There was some discussion of using it in an attempt to salvage the *Lusitania,* but this expedition did not develop. We know today, based upon the work of Robert Ballard, that the *Lusitania* lies in waters far too deep for the salvage tube to reach. The fate of the English salvage tube is unknown, but in all probability it was sold for scrap when Lake began to suffer severe financial problems some years later. The American tube, the *Argosy,* however, was built, and Lake would use it in the final treasure hunt of his life, the search for HMS *Hussar.* He also employed the tube to successfully salvage a large steam dredge belonging to the Bridgeport Dredging Company which sank on July 6, 1920.[10]

For a number of years, Lake had been convinced that there existed a market for a submarine passenger service that would let the public view the marvels of undersea life. With this thought in mind, he began refurbishing the *Defender,* a military submarine he had constructed in 1907 and had been unable to sell. He wanted to provide sight-seeing tours in and around Palm Beach, Miami, Nassau, and Bermuda, figuring he would earn about five hundred dollars per day from such excursions. However, the *Defender* lay dormant in Bridgeport Harbor, never providing a single

fig. 22. Stages in the construction of a Sunshine Home. Courtesy Jeffrey Lake

tour of the ocean's bottom. A few years later he would consider using this craft in another underwater foray: the first attempt to explore the underwater environment of the North Pole.[11]

During this period, Lake had an encounter with the son of his major competitor, John P. Holland, Jr. It seems that young Holland desired to become involved in submarine construction and had in his possession plans that his father had drafted after leaving the Electric Boat Company. He wanted to enlist Lake's assistance in backing his enterprise. Lake's answer was empathetic: "Replying to your favor of February 11th, I can sympathize with your feelings regarding getting something out of the submarine boat business, as I know something of the treatment which was accorded your father and which is common to the lot of most inventors."[12] Lake's busy schedule did not permit the two to meet, and the possibility of binding together the two major submarine families did not materialize.

The year 1929 was a bad one for the United States and the rest of the industrialized world. On October 28, "Black Friday," the stock market collapsed, initiating a world monetary crisis. U.S. securities lost $26 billion in value, throwing the country into a severe economic depression. Average Americans found themselves either out of work or laboring under reduced wages. Simon Lake, a man who valued his work more than he did money, would begin a downward financial spiral. At a time when many were lost in inactivity, Lake seemed to take on an increasing workload. Because of his long interest in manned flight, he was elected to the board of directors of the Kucher Airplane Corporation, a company about which little is known.[13] He was also involved with John Reed, son of Walter Reed, the famed army surgeon and bacteriologist. John was interested in building or purchasing a submarine for a group of South Americans.[14] The outcome of this venture is unknown. Lake had also designed and patented a transoceanic destroyer that operated on the hydroplane principle.[15] The rapid pace of life he was keeping caught up with him, and he suffered a severe bout of neuritis that required him to have twenty teeth extracted.[16]

Lake had begun implementing his underwater sight-seeing enterprise with his old friend, Captain Sloan Danenhower, the year before the stock market crash. They were in the process of refurbishing the twenty-five-year-old *Defender* when they learned that George Palmer Putnam (of the G. P. Putnam and Sons publishing company and husband of Amelia Earhart) was considering the funding of a submarine voyage to the North Pole. Lake and Danenhower contacted Putnam and suggested he consider using the only privately owned submarine in the world, the *Defender*. Apparently, Putnam liked the idea, and the company *Lake and Danenhower Inc.* was formed.

Before the *Defender* would be permitted to sail, the two partners were required to demonstrate to the U.S. Navy that the *Defender* was indeed seaworthy. This required numerous repairs and several shakedown cruises—and another episode with an enemy from Lake's past, Lawrence Y. Spear, former navy constructor and vice president of the Electric Boat Company.[17]

The Navy had placed Lieutenant Commander Palmer H. Dunbar in charge of the *Defender's* tests. In a conversation with Dunbar, Spear indicated that he would libel the *Defender* on her arrival at the submarine base at New London, Connecticut. Lake thought that this rumor had been started because Electric Boat was in the middle of building a diving bell for submarine rescue and Spear may have been working under the assumption that Lake was trying to horn in on the development. He, in fact, was. While refurbishing the *Defender,* Lake signed a contract with the navy to test her diver's chamber as a possible method of rescuing sailors from sunken submarines.[18] The impetus for this work had been the sinking of the S-4 in 1926. That submarine had been rammed while running at periscope depth and went to the bottom with all hands. When the S-4 was finally raised, investigators found that many of the crew had survived for about three days, finally succumbing to asphyxiation. Had the submarine been equipped with Lake's patented diver's chamber, the crew could have been rescued in about three hours.[19]

To Spear's chagrin, no legal grounds were ever identified for a libel suit. However, Dunbar's attitude toward the Lake-Danenhower enterprise was adversely affected and the tests on the *Defender* went awry, often showing what appeared to be sabotage. It seemed to be another case of déjà vu for Lake in his dealings with naval personnel and individuals associated with the Electric Boat Company.[20]

The *Defender* was finally approved by the navy, but shortly thereafter the opportunity to lease an even newer submarine, the O-12 (which had been built by the Lake Torpedo Boat Company and commissioned in 1918) was offered to him by the navy. Lake took advantage of this offer (a lease costing $1 per year), and the O-12 was refurbished and rechristened the *Nautilus*. It would be the first submarine to undertake the arduous task of reaching the North Pole underwater.

CHAPTER 9

North to the Pole

What's the good of Mercators, North Poles and
        Equators,
Tropics, Zones and Meridian Lines?
So the Bellman would cry: and the crew would reply,
They are merely conventional signs.

—*Lewis Carroll*

In 1898 Simon Lake presented a lecture before the faculty of the Johns Hopkins University. He was in an elated state because he had just completed his thousand-mile voyage in the *Argonaut* I, and during his presentation he could not help prophesying the future of the submarine. The prognostication included a short discussion of the work of the Norwegian Arctic explorer Fridtjof Nansen, who had just returned from eighteen months on the arctic ice. Nansen had shown that the ice covering the region was no more than fourteen feet thick. Lake hypothesized that a submarine, equipped with runners, could skate its way under the ice all the way to the North Pole. The idea may have seem far-fetched at the time, considering the primitive state of the submarine, but for an inventor, the impossible is simply that which has not yet been done.[1] Besides, Lake's spiritual mentor, Jules Verne, had his Captain Nemo passing his fictitious submarine below the polar ice on a regular basis. Nemo prophetically stated, "Who knows if in another 100 years we may not see a second Nautilus."[2] In point of fact, in less that one hundred years there would be two submarines named the *Nautilus* headed to the pole. The first *Nautilus*, Lake's converted O-12, would demonstrate the feasibility of under-ice travel in 1931. The second, the atomic submarine *Nautilus*, would reach the pole at 11:15 P.M. on August 3, 1958.

Heading up the 1931 expedition was Sir Hubert Wilkins, a renowned adventurer originally from the outback of southern Australia. His first adventure of note was the photographic documentation of the Balkan War of 1912. He had accompanied Vilhjalmur Stefansson on the 1913 Canadian expedition to the Arctic, but upon learning of war with Germany, Wilkins left the expedition and made his way over the ice to Ottawa and then returned to Australia, where he immediately joined the Australian Flying Corps. He served as a combat photographer in France and established a record as a fearless pilot, being wounded several times and, once, being buried by shellfire. He would go on to many other exploits, including an epic twenty-two-hour flight over the Arctic from Alaska to Spitsbergen, Norway, with Ben Eielson in 1928. This flight was hailed for its daring as well as for its outcome of linking America and Europe across a previously unexplored route. For this feat, he was knighted. Wilkins also led the Wilkins-Hearst Antarctic Expedition that same year, thus becoming the first explorer to have flown over both polar regions.

Wilkins could trace his ancestry to Bishop John Wilkins, who resided in Chester, England, during the seventeenth century. He and Robert Boyle were the cofounders of the Royal Society of London. The good bishop had theorized about submarines propelled by oars and steered with fins. His paper entitled "Concerning the Possibility of Framing an Ark for Submarine Navigation" was published in 1648. In it, he proclaimed the submarine as the best method to reach the North Pole.[3] It appeared that submarines flowed within the Wilkins blood.

Sir Hubert Wilkins and his wife, Suzanne, boarded the *Graf Zeppelin* at Lakehurst, New Jersey, on June 2, 1930, to visit their friend Lincoln Ellsworth in Switzerland. Wilkins's meeting with Ellsworth was for the purpose of enticing the latter to join the polar expedition. Ellsworth was an engineer and aviator who had worked in Alaska, Canada, and South America. He had accompanied Ronald Amundsen (the first to reach the South Pole in 1911) during his flight across the North Pole in 1926. Wilkins and Ellsworth now planned to reach the pole by submarine. They believed that such an expedition would also provide for the exploration of the Arctic between Spitsbergen, northern Greenland, the northern coast of Siberia, Alaska, and the North Pole. In addition, the expedition would permit them to determine the feasibility of using a submarine as a floating weather station. The voyage north would be known as the Wilkins-Ellsworth Expedition and be funded primarily by George Putnam.[4] There are indications that William Randolph Hearst also wanted to back the expedition, but Putnam would not hear of it.[5]

Exactly how Wilkins decided to use the expertise of Simon Lake is unknown. It is quite possible that Lake's reputation had preceded him, as he was the only one with any under-ice submarine experience at the time. In addition to having published numerous articles on the subject, Lake had demonstrated that he could navigate below an ice pack. During the naval trials of the *Protector* in 1903–1904, he had not only traveled below the ice but also demonstrated that a submarine could easily break through the ice from below to reach the surface, provided the thickness of the ice was not excessive. He had patented a specialized drilling device (No. 638,342) that permitted a submarine's crew to bore through thick ice to obtain fresh air for breathing and the running of her engines for recharging her batteries. A second vent in the drill housing allowed for the expulsion of fouled air and exhaust.[6] Lake had also experimented with runners in 1903 (his "inverted toboggan," as he referred to it) to determine whether a submarine could literally skate on the undersurface of the ice when the craft was provided with a small amount of positive buoyancy. The device worked perfectly. He also tried using guide wheels for the same purpose.

Lake had estimated that a trip under the pole would require ten days in complete comfort. The submarine he was proposing would be able to make 150 miles on a single battery charge. In addition to his ice drill, to provide access to the atmosphere for charging his batteries and restoring the air within the submarine, Lake proposed to carry small mines that could be detonated under the ice to blow an opening so the craft could reach the surface.[7]

Originally, Lake and his new partner, Captain Sloan Danenhower, had suggested the use of the refurbished *Defender* for the Wilkins-Ellsworth expedition, but, when the lease of the newer O-12 from the U.S. Navy became available, Lake recommended they take it. After completion of the expedition, the submarine was to be returned to the navy, at which time it would be scrapped. The O-12 was taken to the Philadelphia Navy Yard for repair and outfitting. The expedition members hoped she would be ready for December. Problems with an engine caused a delay, and the submarine was towed to the Brooklyn Navy Yard for repairs. Finally, on March 24, 1931, in the shadow of the Brooklyn Bridge and in the presence of eight hundred spectators, the O-12 was christened *Nautilus*. The honor of christening the submarine was bestowed upon Wilkins's wife, Suzanne,

fig. 23. Early experiments with the *Protector* to demonstrate the feasibility of under-ice travel. From *International Marine Engineering*, 1916.

but the traditional champagne bottle had to be replaced by a silver bucket of ice; Prohibition was in effect. Attending the ceremony was Jean Jules Verne, grandson of the famed science fiction writer. Also present was Hugo Eckner, commander of the *Graf Zeppelin*. Wilkins had tentatively arranged for the airship to rendezvous with the *Nautilus* at the North Pole and to exchange mail as a "demonstration of man's complete mastery of the top of the world." The naval band played the national anthems of Britain, France, and the United States. Standing with the celebrities at the launch was Simon Lake. Wilkins described the scene as follows:

> The other old-timer was the grey-bearded naval architect, Simon Lake, now nearly sixty-five, who had designed and built the first practical submarines before the turn of the century. Many years before the christening day of our *Nautilus,* Simon Lake had smashed one of his submarines up through a foot of ice in Narragansett Bay to prove to skeptics of the United States Navy that it could be done. Now he stood silent, too overcome with emotion to speak, but I knew he took a keen pride in the accomplishments of the undersea craft of which he, more than any other man in the world, was the father.[8]

The *Nautilus* was small by the standards of the day, only 175 feet in length, displacing 560 tons and designed to operate at a depth of 200 feet. She was powered by two 500-horsepower diesel engines, providing a range on the surface of seven thousand miles without refueling. Underwater, she could make 125 miles before her Exide batteries would require recharging. In addition to the long runners over her superstructure, the bow was equipped with a pneumatic shock absorber. The submarine also had two 5,000-watt lights (to illuminate the underside of the ice) and a collapsible periscope and radio antennas. The bow was equipped with Lake's characteristic diving chamber, through which bottom samples would be taken as part of the scientific studies being conducted by the renowned oceanographer Harold Sverdrup.[9]

When announcements of the expedition were first made, the organizers were besieged with requests from people wanting to become members of the crew. Although many of the requests were from qualified individuals, there were several from crackpots. One man, for example, volunteered so that, should the submarine become lodged in the ice, he could be released from the submarine in a steel cylinder. His plan was to be picked up by a whaler and thus become the sole survivor who would describe the fate of the expedition! Some newspapers began referring to the expedition as the "Suicides' Club." From a scientific standpoint, however, the expedition had received strong support from such organizations as the Carnegie Institution, the American Geographical Society, and the Woods Hole Oceanographic Institution on Cape Cod, Massachusetts. Walt Disney also became involved, sending Wilkins a cartoon showing Mickey Mouse waving from a midget submarine.[10]

The *Nautilus* departed from Provincetown, Massachusetts, for the Atlantic on June 4, 1931. Captain Sloan Danenhower was at the helm. About a thousand miles out, the expedition's problems began. During a heavy gale, one of the two diesel engines quit. Shortly thereafter, the second engine began acting up and the crew found that seawater had mixed with the fuel because of a defective sea valve. With a great deal of difficulty and a marked amount of danger, one of the crew was able to saw the fuel intake pipe to a length above the sea water in the fuel tank. This settled the problem until the armature on the generator went to pieces, showering sparks that threatened to set the submarine on fire. The fire was extinguished, but Danenhower felt it necessary to send out an SOS. The call was answered by the American battleships *Arkansas* and *Wyoming*. The *Wyoming* towed the *Nautilus* to Cobb, Ireland, where temporary repairs were made. Added difficulties required the submarine to be placed in dry dock in Plymouth, England. Finally, on August 19, the expedition was ready for the trip to Spitsbergen, but the delays had so altered the time table that they would be attempting their under-ice adventure as the Arctic winter was setting in. The decision was made to make a go of it, and the *Nautilus* was headed north.[11]

As they reached the polar ice, disaster struck once again. Preparations had been made to dive under the ice. As Danenhower eased the controls forward, the *Nautilus* refused to respond. Diver Frank Crilley was sent over the side, the first man to dive below Arctic waters. The news he returned with was not good. Somehow, both diving rudders had broken away. How these rudders were lost without affecting the steering rudder remains a mystery to this day. Thanks to the versatility of the Lake design, the submarine was still capable of diving. However, the trip under the pole was now in serious jeopardy. They had traveled five thousand miles and were within six hundred miles of the pole, and the whole world was waiting in anticipation. In their heads they recognized that the voyage under the pole was lost, but in their hearts they decided to try to navigate under the ice flows anyway. Then the Arctic weather took hold, raising more havoc for the submarine. The casing on a battery cracked during recharging. Apparently, the rapid change in temperature from near zero to the higher temperature that occurred during the recharging was more than the battery could sustain. The resulting chemical fumes rapidly filled the submarine, and Danenhower was forced to head to the surface to vent the poisonous gases. Shortly after this emergency was handled, the oceanographer Harold Sverdrup, responsible for making the first Arctic soundings and collecting samples from the bottom, came scrambling up from the diver's chamber. The severe weather had caused rivets to pop in the chamber, which was now flooding. With difficulty, the crew attempted to plug the leaks, but this proved to be futile. The inner door to the diver's chamber had to be permanently sealed. Bit by bit, the expedition was falling apart.[12]

After considerable discussion, Wilkins and Danenhower decided to attempt the first dive under the Arctic ice. Danenhower's major concern was whether the vents through which the ballast water was blown would freeze over, preventing them from surfacing. Since the water temperature was above freezing, he gave the order to dive. The *Nautilus* nosed down and headed for the ice. Danenhower cut the engines and the submarine began to rise slowly. A resounding crunching sound echoed through the

fig. 24. The *Nautilus* at the start of her polar expedition. From Lake Torpedo Boat Company, *The Development of the Lake Type Submarine* (Bridgeport, Conn.: Lake Torpedo Boat Company, 1910)

craft as she came to rest against the underbelly of the Arctic. The *Nautilus's* depth gauge read thirty-seven feet, indicating that above them was seventeen feet of frozen water.

The view through the conning tower portholes was astoundingly beautiful. For the first time in history, a submarine was under the Arctic ice. The excitement, however, was short-lived, for the explorers now became concerned with whether they would be able to get out from under their icy world. Danenhower ordered the sub full astern. Slowly, and to the relief of everyone on board, the *Nautilus* began to creep from under the ice. Had the submarine lodged there, the crew would have been in dire straits because the ice drill had somehow become jammed.[13]

During the next few weeks, the *Nautilus* made several under-ice dives, and the crew was able to gather a good deal of scientific information. Sverdrup demonstrated four alternating layers of cold and warm water in the Arctic. Numerous water and bottom samples were collected for study once the expedition returned. But the season was growing late, and it was time to move out of the Arctic. During the first week of September, 1931, the *Nautilus* began its homeward trek.

The expedition had failed to reach the pole but had demonstrated the feasibility of under-ice travel and research. Simon Lake was elated and foresaw the day when submarines would regularly cruise under the pole for commercial purposes and mail delivery. His idea for cargo-carrying submarines traveling the polar route, although still not yet a reality, may still come to pass as adventurers continue to explore "inner space." Hubert Wilkins lived to see the atomic *Nautilus* reach the pole in 1958.

CHAPTER 10

The Search for
HMS *Hussar*

Thou Greybeard, old Wisdom, mayst boast
    of thy treasures;
Give me with young Folly to live;
I grant thee calm-blooded, time-settled pleasures.
                                    —*Robert Burns*

She sailed out of New York Harbor heading for Long Island Sound and Newport, Rhode Island, through the dangerous narrows known as Hell Gate. On board the British frigate HMS *Hussar* were a full crew and fifty-four American prisoners chained in irons below deck. The year was 1780, and the British troops were being forced to evacuate New York by the colonial American army. Newport was still under the protection of the British fleet, and the English had decided to establish a paymaster's headquarters in Newport after the fall of New York. According to various sources, the *Hussar* carried a million-dollar payroll in gold and silver specie for the British troops. Other sources estimate the value of the cargo to be worth over one million pounds. As the ship neared Stoney Point, she struck an underwater obstacle called Pot Rock and began to take on water. The captain, attempting to prevent the loss of his ship, ordered out a long hawser, which was tied to a large tree. The weight of the sinking vessel, however, was too much for the tree to sustain, and it was ripped out by its roots as the ship sank stern first in twelve fathoms of water. The adjacent trees would, in time, become known as the *Hussar* trees and mark the site of the ship's demise. Many of the crew drowned, as did all of the American prisoners.[1]

The rumor of sunken treasure on the *Hussar* spawned numerous salvaging attempts. Shortly after a peace was reached with the colonies, the English reportedly sent two expeditions to try to reach her, but the strong currents in Hell Gate and the primitive state of salvaging equipment prevented divers from reaching the wreck. As a boy in 1884, Simon Lake had watched the crew of the steamer *Chester* pumping mud onto screens from which golden guineas were reportedly being retrieved. There was a Captain Thomas of Orange, New Jersey, who in 1897 told Lake of sending a man to England where he learned that a large sum of money had been hidden with the ballast of the *Hussar*. Further, Thomas claimed that one of the two English expeditions had attempted to use a diving bell to reach the wreck. Again, little was salvaged because of the swift currents. Thomas had spent several years working the site under a contract from the secretary of the Treasury, but like the others, he had been unable to find any of the treasure.

Lake had obtained statements from Captain Charles W. Pratt and Captain L. W. Bancroft of Worcester, Massachusetts, the last salvagers to work on the *Hussar*. They reported tearing up portions of the ship's deck and removing parts of many skeletons. Some leg bones still had shackles on them. They also retrieved a few gold coins, two of which Captain Bancroft had fashioned into breast pins for his daughters. A cannon salvaged from the wreck is still on display at the Worcester Museum, in Worcester, Massachusetts. They were, however, unable to reach the main hold of the ship.[2] Lake had also spoken with divers who had worked for Pratt and Bancroft and learned that they could spend only about fifteen minutes on the site during slack tides, a factor that seriously hindered their search. In a letter from another diver who had worked on the *Hussar* salvage, Lake learned that "he absolutely [had] seen the gold, been on the ship and handled [it], and for reasons best known to himself, left it there, but he is planning to go back after it."[3]

Subsequently, Lake found on file with the U.S. Treasury Department a letter from England written by the Captain of the *Hussar* shortly after her sinking and containing the following statement: "I am not aware that there was any treasure on board her or anything but stores belonging to her as a twenty-eight gun ship."[4] If accurate, the letter would lay waste to claims that the British frigate was a treasure ship. However, many people thought that this letter was a ploy to keep the Yanks from attempting her salvage. If, indeed, the treasure did not exist, what was the reason for the two British salvaging expeditions? Whatever the truth, the situation seemed right out of a Jules Verne novel, and the perfect sort of stimulus for a man like Simon Lake. As he contemplated the operation in 1934, he seemed, at the time, more consumed with resuming his salvaging business than beginning a treasure hunt. In a letter to a friend, he wrote:

> Did the Hussar carry any treasure? and if so, was any of it ever recovered? Frankly, I would not spend much time or money to find out, and I at first regretted that my communications with the Treasury Department asking for a contract to try to find her, ever became public, but it brought me a lot of interesting information, pro and con about her and now I have decided to clear up these mysteries once and for all by spending a few days with my new type of Submarine Apparatus, which will relieve us of the dangers and difficulty of diving in a swift current, and enable anyone to go down directly into her old hulk and clean her out to her inner planking . . .[5]

His ambivalence would undergo significant change, and the "few days" would lengthen into three years.

Simon Lake was not a man who would or could sit still for very long. While the Wilkins-Ellsworth polar expedition was in progress, Lake had built a new salvage tube. Like his original *Argosy* and the English tube he had constructed for salvaging the *Lutine* treasure, his new creation consisted of a mother ship (the *Lillian*), to which one end of the tube was articulated, the other end locking onto a submarine chamber (called the *Laksco*). This strange contraption was launched on October 6, 1934, from the Housatonic Shipbuilding Company, located on the Housatonic River in Stratford, Connecticut. She was christened by his granddaughter, Miss Winifred Eger Lake, with the traditional champagne bottle broken over the hull (Prohibition having been repealed in 1933). At the launch Lake stated for the press, "I believe this craft is destined to prove that there are greater opportunities lying under the surface of the seas for future exploration and development than are above water. Most of the areas above the surface of the sea have already been explored and largely developed, while the large areas beneath the sea are capable of growing more edible food stuffs per acre than exist above the sea."[6] Lake, at the age of sixty-eight, had returned to his original, Jules Verne–inspired reason for building his submarines: undersea exploration and salvaging.

The initial search for the *Hussar* began with a series of test borings along the western shore of the East River in New York. Lake had focused

fig. 25. Lake's salvage tube, *Argonaut*, with her mother ship, *Argosy*, during her shakedown cruise. From Submarine Exploration and Recovery Company, *Recovering the Natural Resources of the Sea* (Bridgeport, Conn.: Submarine Exploration and Recovery Company, 1920)

his attention on an area between 132nd Street and south of the Triborough Bridge to 86th Street. Shortly thereafter, the *Lillian* and *Laksco* were brought to the river and a bottom search commenced. To demonstrate that his salvage tube could, in fact, locate and raise sunken cargoes, Lake found the remains of a barge in Long Island Sound and pumped ten tons of anthracite coal form her bowels.[7]

On September 26, 1936, the *Bridgeport Post* announced: "Simon Lake Strikes Gold under Hell Gate; Millions Lost 156 Years Ago to Be Salvaged." Lake had located what he thought was the deck of the *Hussar* under twelve feet of silt. He was careful to explain to reporters that he did not know whether the treasure was still there, and, always the dreamer, he half-heartedly suggested the idea of raising the frigate for display at the 1939 World's Fair. The press was having a field day with the story. Meanwhile, Lake began the expensive and time-consuming process of clearing the site. To his dismay, he would learn that his press releases and plans were premature.[8]

While the *Hussar* venture progressed, Lake began the construction of another underwater research craft. Variously called the "Crab," the "baby

ON THE SEA-FLOOR WITHOUT DIVING DRESS: A SALVAGE SUBMARINE.

The above view is from a photo of the "Argosy and Argonaut" reproduced from "The Illustrated London News"—drawing by courtesy of "The Scientific American" and photos by Underwood & Underwood. Central drawing is a very good illustration of the surface boat with a man climbing up to the surface from the submarine, through the access tube and another man in the diving compartment picking up articles from the bottom. Upper right hand photo shows a lady passenger just coming up from a trip to the bottom with her "catch", a horseshoe crab and a flat fish; lower left photo is a view of the submarine and tube from the surface vessel.

fig. 26. Artist's conception of the salvage tube. From Submarine Exploration and Recovery Company, *Recovering the Natural Resources of the Sea* (Bridgeport, Conn.: Submarine Exploration and Recovery Company, 1920)

fig. 27. The rusting hulk of the *Laksco* in Milford Harbor, Milford, Connecticut. Courtesy William E. Poluhowich

sub," a "salt-water flivver," or his "vest-pocket " submarine, his new craft was formally named the *Explorer*. This submarine measured twenty-two feet in length with a seven-foot beam, weighed ten tons, and was designed to operate as deep as three hundred feet. As with many of Lake's designs, she was equipped with wheels for crawling over the sea bottom. This baby submarine was a combination of submersible and salvage tube, the craft retaining an umbilical linkage to its mother ship, which supplied fresh air and power. Projecting from her bow was a mechanical grab that was operated from within the submarine. She also had Lake's patented diving chamber for direct access to the ocean's floor. The *Explorer* was designed for the commercial recovery of minerals, sponges, shellfish, and other riches of the sea. As was typical of Lake's enthusiasm for his inventions, he predicted that this submarine would provide easy access to the ocean for numerous industries and proposed creating another shipbuilding plant in Connecticut to produce these craft. His estimated cost for the *Explorer* was fifteen thousand dollars.[9]

The *Explorer* generated interest in many circles. Commercial sponge fishermen in Florida expressed an interest, as did a number of mining companies. Lake was especially proud of the interest shown by the deep-sea explorer Dr. William Beebe. In September of 1932, Beebe had reached a depth of 2,200 feet in his cast-iron sphere he called the "bathysphere." Two years later, he and Otis Barton would descend to a record depth of 3,028 feet.[10] Beebe's interest in the *Explorer* stemmed from his desire to use her for underwater photography, and Beebe probably would have used the submarine had it ever reached Florida as Lake had proposed. But the treasure hunt in New York delayed the *Explorer*'s transport south. Lake decided to use his vest-pocket submarine to search the bottom of the East River because, by this time, he realized that he had not located the *Hussar*. Instead, he had uncovered another vessel that had met her doom in Hell Gate. Beebe did have an opportunity to inspect the *Explorer* while she lay in New York Harbor. The submarine, however, was to play only a minor role in the treasure hunt because by 1937 Lake was running into serious financial difficulties.

In an attempt to pay off creditors and keep his companies solvent, Lake sold some personal property. He held several auctions in his home on Milford's green. Paintings, rugs, furniture, and other items garnered over a lifetime of living on two continents—and worth thousands of dollars—sold for hundreds. The financial pressures became so great that Lake was threatened with foreclosure on his beautiful colonial home because he was unable to satisfy debts totaling $12,045. The Forsberg Manufacturing Company, which had taken over the Seaview Avenue site of the Lake Torpedo Boat Company, filed a writ of attachment against *Explorer* for $784 as payment for mooring fees.[11] Financial problems grew until, finally, on December 30, 1938, Lake lost his beloved home. It was sold to George J. Smith and Sons, who converted the mansion into a funeral home.[12] Lake and his wife, Margaret, moved into a modest home two doors down from

fig. 28. William Beebe inspects the *Explorer* in New York Harbor (*top;* courtesy Thomas A. E. Lake); the *Explorer* in her new berth in Milford, Connecticut (*bottom;* courtesy Grace Glenn)

their former "big house." It would be in their new residence that the inventor and his wife would celebrate their fiftieth wedding anniversary in 1940.[13]

If the *Hussar* treasure existed at all, it still resides in the polluted waters of the East River. Lake was forced to call off the search on June 24, 1937, after three years of searching for the remains of the old frigate. His reward? Eighty-six cents. Like so many treasure hunts, past, present, and future, more "treasure" is made by the creditors than by the seekers. When interviewed about his failure to find his treasure ship, Lake, undaunted as ever, indicated that he intended to continue the search in the near future. He stated, "There is still an area under the 13th Street pier which has not been explored. According to an old chart I have, that would be the most likely spot for the captain of the Hussar to have headed, for his old sailing ship was leaking badly."[14] He would never return to treasure hunting in Hell Gate. Instead, the feisty inventor turned his efforts toward several other endeavors.

A historical footnote is required here. On September 19, 1985, a newspaper release indicated that salvager Barry Clifford form Massachusetts had found the *Hussar*. Like Simon Lake, Clifford was cautious in his public statement. "It's not a sure thing," he said, "but I wouldn't be out here if I didn't believe there wasn't something on the Hussar." And, just as Simon Lake had provided evidence for the existence of the treasure and laid plans for its recovery almost fifty years before, Clifford went on to say, "But one man reported seeing 14 wagons of gold loaded onto the ship 205 years ago, shortly before it left Lower Manhattan . . . [the hope is] to raise the craft and have it displayed somewhere in the New York area, possibly at the South Street Seaport."[15] The echo was all too familiar. And so were the results. To this day, the *Hussar* still remains in her watery grave; her treasure, if in fact it really exists, still eludes its seekers.

CHAPTER 11

Dust

There is no lamp for the path of the future except the experience of the past.

—Patrick Henry

The sweet remembrances of the just
Shall flourish when he sleeps in the dust.

—Psalm 112: 6

In August of 1938, Simon Lake received an urgent call from a member of the Dodge family. The wealthy automobile manufacturing family learned had that their son, Daniel G. Dodge, had drowned on August 15 after having been involved in a dynamite blast in Georgian Bay, Canada. A week-long search had not been able to locate the body. Sparing no expense, the family requested Lake to transport his *Explorer* to Canada to search for the body. The project required Lake to make special arrangements for the railroad passage because of the submarine's weight. This was hardly a problem for Lake in light of his experiences with submarine transport in Russia. He was ready to go in ten days. As the craft was being loaded onto a flatcar, news came that the body had been found. This would be the last adventure for the *Explorer*. It would also be Simon Lake's last underwater endeavor.[1]

World War II broke out in Europe in 1939, and the submarine began to play the major role Lake had predicted. By 1940, the seventy-four-year-old inventor was back in Washington trying to convince government officials of the advantages of cargo-carrying submarines. Lake made a direct appeal to President Franklin D. Roosevelt for his transport submarines. He reminded the president of the successful evasion of the British blockade by the German cargo carrier *Deutschland* and extolled her ability to safely carry large cargoes undetected across the Atlantic. Lake also pointed out that the *Deutschland* was small in comparison with his original designs that had been employed by the Germans to build their cargo carrier. He argued: "We can build undersea craft which will be as large and as comfortable as surface ships. We can have them hold more than 1,000 people. I wrote to Lord Balfour in 1921 suggesting experiments along this line."[2] His pleas were falling on deaf ears. The various subcommittees he testified before opted for the use of ship convoys to counter the German U-boat menace in the Atlantic Ocean and North Sea. Most members of the committees Lake dealt with considered the undersea freighters too costly, even though Lake was able to show that a decreased loss of shipping (because his cargo carriers were, at the time, virtually undetectable) actually represented a very substantial savings of money. When one views the total tonnage lost during the war, it appears that Lake might have been correct in his assumptions.[3]

Lake also argued to Congress and the news media that the submarine represented a cost-effective method for coastal defense, and he designed a fleet of unique submarines to demonstrate this point. He modified the characteristic wheels on his submarines for direct transport of the craft over railroad tracks. His ingenious plan called for mobile submarines that could be brought rapidly by rail to numerous ports and be launched wherever needed for coastal defense. The proposal was again lost somewhere in the Washington shuffle.[4]

Apparently, Lake reestablished the attitude he had developed during his first encounter with Washington bureaucrats and decided to build his cargo carrier without the assistance of the government. So began a number of trips to Richmond, Virginia, to visit J. Louis Reynolds, vice president of the Reynolds Metals Company. His proposal was for an undersea freighter capable of carrying up to 7,500 tons of cargo or as many as 2,500 troops. Unfortunately, this project never reached fruition. It was during this time that Lake suffered his first heart attack.

While recovering, Lake and his son Tom turned their attention to hydroplane boats, surface vessels that could attain high speeds by riding on hull extensions that reduced surface contact with the hull. In the archives of the Submarine Library and Museum in New London, Connecticut, is a film showing Tom racing their prototype boat up and down the Housatonic River in Stratford, Connecticut. The small, one-man craft laid much of the groundwork for today's high-speed racing and military hydroplane vessels.

On June 23, 1945, at the age of seventy-nine, Simon Lake died of a heart attack. He left behind his wife, Margaret, his son, Thomas Alva Edison Lake, two daughters, Miriam and Margaret, and a legacy that, for the most part, has gone unheralded. Except for certain naval texts, few history books recount his exploits. There are no monuments or statues to commemorate his contributions, save a grammar school in Milford, Connecticut, that bears his name. His pocket submarine, *Explorer,* resides at the public library in Milford, Connecticut, and the hulk of the *Laksco* lies rusting in Milford Harbor. These are the only remnants of a lifetime of work. At the Seaview Avenue site of the Lake Torpedo Boat Company in Bridgeport, Connecticut, the rotting ways from which his submarines were launched bear stark testimony to Simon Lake's contributions to naval history. Few of the city's residents are aware of their significance.

Today, most naval historians agree that Simon Lake made significant contributions to the development and acceptance of the submarine as both a military weapon and a research vehicle. Many of the features on his submarines for which he was credited were not original. Even-keel diving, hydroplanes, drop keels, wheels, and the diver's chamber, for example, had been employed in earlier submarines. Lake's contribution was the successful incorporation of *all* these devices into his submarines, thereby producing versatile craft that accomplished the goals he sought. Although he was considered by many as the father of the modern submarine, Lake dismissed this moniker as presumptuous. However, his success as an underwater salvager and undersea explorer should serve to establish him as the father of modern undersea exploration.

Lake held over 200 patents, 111 of which dealt with submarines. Twenty-five were still important components in submarines built during the Second World War, and it would not be surprising to find many of these incorporated in our modern atomic fleet (a number of Lake's personal papers in the National Archives remain classified).[5] There can be little doubt that Simon Lake contributed significantly to the early development of the Russian submarine force, which, until the end of the Cold War, was recognized as one of the most formidable forces in the world. In a similar manner, he assisted Germany in its development of submarines, although his actual contributions have been shrouded by the industrial espionage that ran rampant through his European plant just prior to the onset of the First World War. The successful employment of the German submarine cargo carrier *Deutschland*, which was constructed from his designs, attests, in part, to his contributions to the German submarine effort. Although shunned in his initial efforts to construct submarines for his own government, his persistence was finally rewarded when he succeeded in gaining the acceptance that permitted him to operate a very successful submarine building program during World War I.

Simon Lake was a versatile individual. This versatility may have produced the impression that he was somewhat of a gadfly, jumping from one project to another, seemingly unrelated, throughout his lifetime. In reality, he was attempting to satisfy an immense curiosity, particularly that for the underwater environment that had been inspired in him by the books of his spiritual mentor, Jules Verne. He was a talented inventor and a self-taught engineer who was tenacious once he had identified a problem. He had a knack for thinking through and seeking a solution to any problem that caught his fancy, be it a military submarine or the search for sunken treasure. These traits made it common for him to juggle several different, often unrelated projects simultaneously. At any given time, his desk might be littered with submarine designs mixed with such things as plans for concrete homes or cement pipes. He was a much better inventor than businessman. His friend Frank Miller, president of the City National Bank of Bridgeport, once remarked, "I have known Simon for years and I am fond of him, but he doesn't know the value of a dollar or how to keep it after he gets it," to which Lake replied, "That's probably true. But I'd rather die broke because I had been spending my money doing worthwhile things, than sit around cutting coupons."[6]

Even after losing the immense fortune he had earned, Lake continued to approach the government with inventions he felt would benefit the country, particularly during World War II. In a confidential letter to the U.S. Navy, he laid out a plan for protecting the American coastline by using an underwater hydrophone system to detect the engine sounds from submarines. Although the government did not take it seriously at the time, today our coasts are, in fact, guarded by just such a system. Strategically placed hydrophones are being used to detect submarines that cruise below one thousand feet as part of SOSUS (the Sound Surveillance System).[7] Such was the foresight of Simon Lake.

The intrepid inventor was a man of his times. Patriotic to the core, his concern and foresight lay in bettering the United States' standing in the world; hence his involvement with military submarines. There was a streak of paranoia in him that most certainly arose from his dealings with the government. It caused him to dwell upon the idea of the "inventor as the underdog."

Lake's thinking reflects a man of temperance, which he was. Certain of his comments provide an insight into his character as well as his trials and tribulations:

> I love the Russians for many things, but those we [i.e., the inventor and his wife] were able to observe were lacking in morals as so many mice . . .

> I did not feel then, I do not feel now—the slightest responsibility for Germany's use of the submarine, but there is no blinking the fact that her boats had been built on my plans . . .

> I do not know precisely how much money the United States owes me and those associated with me. I may never get a penny of it. I feel that we have been most unfairly treated . . .[8]

Many have referred to Simon Lake as the "Father of the Submarine," a title he took exception to. It is clear from Lake's early writings that he aptly realized the maxim that one must build upon the contributions of one's forebears. He was quick to applaud the many brave souls who first attempted to venture below the water's surface. Today, credit for the development of the submarine is most often given to John P. Holland, Lake's major rival. The two inventors provide a study in contrast. John Holland was a man of single purpose. He planned for and built submarines designed specifically as weapons of war. Simon Lake, during his initial and final involvement in submarine construction, saw the submarine as a means of benefiting mankind by harvesting the riches of the sea. His vision was patterned after that of Jules Verne. Paradoxically, his patriotism stifled his vision, and he felt compelled to build military craft. Still, Lake was more concerned with the defensive rather than the offensive aspects of the submarine. He once stated: "I have always considered the submarine in light of a weapon for defensive purposes only, and, as such, believe it is bound to become the premier weapon on which all nations must rely for their defense from an invading force by the sea."[9]

One must ponder what Lake's contributions and reputation would have been in comparison with those of John Holland had he remained a salvager. Both Lake and Holland suffered a paranoia that was established during their interactions with Washington bureaucrats and leaders of industry. Both were honorable men of the highest integrity. Where Holland tended to be quiet and unassuming, Lake seemed to enjoy the spotlight of the news media. Their involvement with the military permitted each to predict upcoming world conflicts—Holland predicting World War I, Lake prophesying World War II. Holland built submarines for speed and stealth. Lake constructed submarines with wheels to prowl the bottom. Of the two inventors, Simon Lake was probably the better known during their lifetimes. An example of his celebrity can be seen in a letter that was sent to him from Europe in 1921. The address on the envelope consisted of no more than a sketch of the noted inventor and the lettering "Bridgeport, Conn." Postal employees immediately recognized the image, and Lake received the letter without delay.[10]

During his lifetime, Lake admitted to only two failures. He was modest enough to state: "I do not mean that everything I have attempted has been a success. I have spent time on ideas that were later dropped for other ideas that were more timely or more interesting. But there has always been something at the root of whatever it was I have been working on. I have gotten out patents and forgotten them. I have started many a rabbit down many a track and let it get away. But I have only failed twice—when I undertook to retire."[11] The first "retirement" occurred in 1915 when the Lake Torpedo Boat Company was operating full tilt and Lake was a wealthy man. It did not take long for idleness to become boring. Regarding the life of leisure, Lake said:

> That cannot be done by Simon Lake, at least. I have never had more all-inclusive misery than while I was trying to live up to my fortune and have a good time. I could not form the habit of loafing. I do not like to play. My feet get tired when I tramp through picture galleries although I can stand on a steel deck all day. I am prey to every form of pest from sand-gnats to black flies. I get sick. I lose interest in things. Until I get back to work I am a total loss.[12]

In 1920, as his company began suffering financial problems, Lake thought again about retiring. He was tired but by no means beaten. He said of this second retirement: "I quit this foolishness about retiring, went back to work, lost all my money, and have been quite happy."[13]

Some may be amused with Simon Lake and see him as a man who provided good theater. Others recognize the innate drive of a creative genius that could not be stifled and ultimately achieved great things. He may be accused of attempting to do too many things in too many different areas of endeavor and, as a result, not achieving recognition in the one

fig. 29. All that remains: the rotting ways in Bridgeport Harbor, Bridgeport, Connecticut, from which Lake's submarines were launched. Courtesy William E. Poluhowich

area he loved the most. However, Simon Lake helped establish a mode of life and an attitude for success that continues today in the inventive spirit of the country that he loved. John Lonnquest has provided the eulogy that best summarizes Simon Lake's contributions:

> From an engineering viewpoint, many of Lake's inventions were responsible for the development of the modern submarine. Lake invented the hydroplane, the principle of even keel descent, the twin configuration superstructure and inner pressure hull, and the first practical periscope. Today every submarine in the world operates using these inventions, but in Lake's day they were new and untried developments. Throughout his long and varied career, Simon Lake influenced the course of submarine development, both in the United States and abroad. In Simon Lake there existed the qualities of inventor, businessman, and lobbyist, which together created a brilliant and dynamic individual. Lake was able to perceive the technical aspects of submarine construction, yet he was also a visionary, capable of imagining men

farming the bottom of the sea. Put together, all of these attributes created an exceptional person. As an individual, Simon Lake was both brilliant and unique, and as an inventor, his submarines changed the course of history.[14]

Simon Lake was a man of many achievements, and his foresight, like that of Jules Verne, will continue to provide inspiration for future generations. It is a shame that Verne did not live to write the story of Simon Lake.

Submarines Constructed for the U.S. Government by the Lake Torpedo Boat Company

Hull Number	Date Launched	Class (Name)	Year Stricken
SS 19 1/2	2-8-1911	*G-1 (Seal)*	1921
SS 27	1-10-1912	*G-2 (Tuna)*	1919
SS 31	12-27-1913	*G-3 (Turbot)*	1922
SS 44	5-1-1916	*L-5*	1925
SS 45	8-31-1916	*L-6*	1925
SS 46	9-26-1916	*L-7*	1925
SS 48	4-23-1917	*L-8*	1925
SS 56	4-27-1916	*N-4*	1922
SS 57	6-13-1918	*N-5*	1922
SS 58	7-9-1918	*N-6*	1922
SS 59	6-15-1918	*N-7*	1922
SS 72	10-29-1917	*O-11*	1930
SS 73	9-29-1917	*O-12*	1930
SS 74	12-27-1917	*O-13*	1930
SS 75	5-6-1918	*O-14*	1930
SS 76	2-12-1918	*O-15*	1930
SS 77	2-9-1918	*O-16*	1930
SS 98	6-17-1919	*R-21*	1930
SS 99	7-10-1918	*R-22*	1930
SS 100	11-15-1918	*R-23*	1930
SS 101	8-21-1918	*R-24*	1930
SS 102	5-15-1919	*R-25*	1930
SS 103	6-28-1919	*R-26*	1930

SS 104	9-23-1918	*R-27*	1930
SS 106	2-15-1919	*S-2*	1931
SS 119	10-22-1919	*S-14*	1945
SS 120	3-8-1920	*S-15*	1946
SS 121	12-23-1919	*S-16*	1945
SS 122	5-22-1920	*S-17*	1945
SS 159	2-26-1921	*S-48*	1946
SS 160	4-23-1921	*S-49*	1931
SS 161	6-18-1921	*S-50*	1931
SS162	8-20-1921	*S-51*	1930

APPENDIX B

Companies Owned
and/or Operated by Simon Lake

The Argonaut Salvage Corporation
Bedrock Gold Submarine-Machinery Company
Connecticut Building and Supply Company
Connecticut Lakeolith Corporation
Deep Sea Submarine Salvage Corporation
Lake & Danenhower Incorporated
Lake Engineering Company, Ltd.
The Lake Submarine Company
The Lake Submarine Salvage Corporation
The Lake Torpedo Boat Company
The Submarine Exploration and Recovery Company
Under Water Recovery Corporation

Notes

Introduction

1. Thomas A. E. Lake, interview with author, Stratford, Conn., July, 1972.

2. Sean Dennis Cashman, *America in the Gilded Age,* 408 pp.

3. Richard Compton-Hall, *Submarine Boats: The Beginnings of Underwater Warfare,* p. 103.

4. Quoted in Simon Lake, *Submarine: The Autobiography of Simon Lake,* p. v.

5. Ibid., pp. 1–196.

6. Lake, interview, July, 1972.

7. Simon Lake, *The Submarine in War and Peace,* pp. 1–297.

8. Murray F. Sueter, *The Evolution of the Submarine Boat, Mine and Torpedo,* pp. 11–135; James B. Sweeney, *A Pictorial History of Oceanographic Submersibles,* pp. 100–106; John C. Lonnquest, "The Role of Simon Lake in the Development of the Modern Submarine" (undergraduate honors thesis, Washington College, 1981), pp. 26–187.

9. Ray Stannard Barker, "Voyaging Under the Sea. I. The Submarine Boat 'Argonaut' and Her Achievements," *McClure's Magazine,* Jan., 1899, pp. 195–209.

Chapter 1. The Pitch Pine Submarine

1. Simon Lake, *Submarine in War and Peace,* pp. 127–30.

2. Simon Lake, *Autobiography,* p. 37.

3. Simon Lake, *Submarine in War and Peace,* pp. 136–38.

4. Simon Lake, "Modern Submarines in War and Peace," *International Marine Engineering,* July, 1915/Apr., 1916, pp. 10–16; Alan H. Burgoyne, *Submarine Navigation, Past and Present,* vol. 1, pp. 225–29.

5. Simon Lake, "Modern Submarines in War and Peace," pp. 14–15.

6. Simon Lake, *Autobiography,* pp. 55–57.

7. Ibid., pp. 59–62.

8. Ibid., p. 62.

9. Lake Submarine Company, Papers of Incorporation.

10. Simon Lake, *Autobiography,* pp. 63–64.

11. *New York Herald,* Jan. 8, 1895, p. 3.

12. Ibid., p. 3.

13. Richard K. Morris, *John P. Holland, 1841–1914: Inventor of the Modern Submarine,* pp. 58–59.

14. Ibid., p. 59; John P. Holland, "Submarine Navigation," *Cassier's Magazine,* vol. 12, 1897, pp. 541–60.

15. Holland, "Submarine Navigation," pp. 541–60; Simon Lake, *Submarine in War and Peace,* vol. 1, pp. 161–62; Lonnquest, "Role of Simon Lake," pp. 43–44.

16. Simon Lake, *Submarine in War and Peace*, p. 121; Burgoyne, *Submarine Navigation*, vol. 1, pp. 100–102, 144–48, 178–82.

17. Simon Lake, *Submarine in War and Peace*, p. 125.

18. Morris, *John P. Holland*, pp. 61–62.

19. Ibid., p. 59.

20. Ibid.

21. Simon Lake, *Submarine in War and Peace*, p. 188; Burgoyne, *Submarine Navigation*, vol. 1, pp. 178–84.

22. Simon Lake, *Submarine in War and Peace*, pp. 163–64; Morris, *John P. Holland*, pp. 109–12.

23. Simon Lake, *Submarine in War and Peace*, pp. 171–76; Burgoyne, *Submarine Navigation*, vol. 1, pp. 260–61; Sueter, *Evolution*, p. 111.

24. Simon Lake, *Submarine in War and Peace*, p. 121; Morris, *John P. Holland*, pp. 67–70.

25. Simon Lake, *Autobiography*, p. 39.

26. Simon Lake, *Submarine in War and Peace*, p. 121.

27. Morris, *John P. Holland*, p. 68.

28. Simon Lake, *Submarine in War and Peace*, p. 125; Morris, *John P. Holland*, pp. 70–74.

29. Simon Lake, *Submarine in War and Peace*, pp. 126–127; Burgyone, *Submarine Navigation*, vol. 1, pp. 244–45.

30. Simon Lake, *Submarine in War and Peace*, pp. 131–35.

31. Ibid., p. 176; Morris, *John P. Holland*, pp. 76–77; John J. Poluhowich, "Bridgeport's Submarine Pioneer," *LISA/86 Festivals Magazine* (*Long Island Sound Festival Magazine*), 1986, pp. 46–48.

Chapter 2. A Craft with a Long History

1. Alex Roland, *Underwater Warfare in the Age of Sail*, pp. 1–5.

2. Sweeney, *Pictorial History*, pp. 13–16.

3. Ibid., pp. 17–18; Burgoyne, *Submarine Navigation*, vol. 1, p. 6; Edward Horton, *The Illustrated History of the Submarine*, pp. 11–12.

4. Burgoyne, *Submarine Navigation*, vol. 1, p. 6; Sweeney, *Pictorial History*, p. 21.

5. Burgoyne, *Submarine Navigation*, vol. 1, pp. 6–8.

6. Sweeney, *Pictorial History*, p. 29.

7. Ibid., pp. 30–31; Burgoyne, *Submarine Navigation*, vol. 1, pp. 6–7.

8. Sweeney, *Pictorial History*, pp. 33–34; Miguel de Cervantes Saavedra, *Don Quixote de la Mancha*, pp. 113–14.

9. Ibid., pp. 40–44.

10. Burgoyne, *Submarine Navigation*, vol. 1, p. 12.

11. Ibid., pp. 12–13.

12. Sweeney, *Pictorial History*, p. 51; Gladys Walker, "From Turtle to Trident," *Connecticut Magazine*, Summer, 1970, pp. 34–40.

13. Sweeney, *Pictorial History*, p. 53.

14. Ibid., pp. 54–56; Burgoyne, *Submarine Navigation*, vol. 1, pp. 12–13; Horton, *Illustrated History*, pp. 8–11.

15. Sweeney, *Pictorial History*, p. 54.

16. Ibid., p. 55.

17. William Barclay Parsons, *Robert Fulton and the Submarine*, pp. vii–ix.

18. Horton, *Illustrated History*, pp. 16–19.

19. Sweeney, *Pictorial History*, pp. 59–64.

20. Parsons, *Robert Fulton and the Submarine*, pp. 25–26.

21. Ibid., pp. 26–27.

22. Ibid., p. 37; M. P. Cocker, *Observer's Directory of the Royal Naval Submarines, 1901–1982,* pp. 11–21.

23. Parsons, *Robert Fulton and the Submarine,* p. 43.

24. Ibid., p. 48.

25. Ibid., p. 86.

26. Sweeney, *Pictorial History,* pp. 63–64.

27. Parsons, *Robert Fulton and the Submarine,* p. 141.

28. Ibid., pp. 141–43.

29. Burgoyne, *Submarine Navigation,* vol. 1, pp. 15–17.

30. Ibid., p. 42.

31. Knut Prenliss, "The American Submarine," manuscript in the National Archives, pp. 1–23.

32. Burgoyne, *Submarine Navigation,* vol. 1, pp. 43–44.

33. Patricia A. Gruse Harris, *Great Lake's First Submarine,* pp. 1–22.

34. Ibid., pp. 23–52.

35. Burgoyne, *Submarine Navigation,* vol. 1, p. 54.

36. Sweeney, *Pictorial History,* pp. 74–82; Burgoyne, *Submarine Navigation,* vol. 1, pp. 53–60.

37. William E. Beard, "The Log of the C. S. Submarine," *Proceedings of the U.S. Naval Institute* 37 (1916): 1546–48; Wilbur Cross, "Last Cruise of the Iron Witch," *True Magazine,* June, 1960, pp. 51–53, 105.

38. Beard, "Log of the C. S. Submarine," pp. 1549–50.

39. Ibid., pp. 1551–53.

40. Ibid., pp. 1554–56.

41. Ibid., p. 1557.

42. "Confederate Sub Sighted" (news brief), *Archaeology,* vol. 48, no. 5 (Sept.–Oct., 1995): 17.

43. Burgoyne, *Submarine Navigation,* vol. 1, pp. 73–74; Sweeney, *Pictorial History,* p. 87.

44. Morris, *John P. Holland,* p. 38.

45. Ibid., pp. 30–31; Burgoyne, *Submarine Navigation,* vol. 2, p. 2.

46. Morris, *John P. Holland,* p. 31.

47. Ibid., p. 38.

48. Ibid., pp. 39–42.

49. Ibid., pp. 40–42.

50. Ibid., pp. 43–44.

51. Burgoyne, *Submarine Navigation,* vol. 2, pp. 1–23.

52. Morris, *John P. Holland,* pp. 50–52.

53. Ibid., pp. 53–58.

54. Roland, *Underwater Warfare,* pp. 1–8.

Chapter 3. The Thousand-Mile Journey

1. Burgoyne, *Submarine Navigation,* vol. 1, p. 247.

2. Simon Lake, *The Argonaut, Her Evolution and History, What She Was Built For and What She Has Accomplished,* pp. 1–32.

3. E. T. Evans, *Dictionary of American Biography, 1941–1945,* pp. 435–37; Cocker, *Observer's Directory,* pp. 11–21; Bernard Grun, *The Timetables of History, 1866–1945.*

4. *National Press Reporter* 16, no. 12, May, 1914, p. 12.

5. Albert Nelson Marquis, *Who's Who in America, 1932–1933,* p. 310.

6. Ibid.; Simon Lake, *Autobiography,* p. 20.

7. Simon Lake, *Autobiography,* p. 10.

8. Ibid., pp. 18–19.

9. Ibid., pp. 161–69.

10. Ibid., pp. 24–25.

11. Ibid., pp. 29–30.

12. Ibid., p. 37.

13. Compton-Hall, *Submarine Boats*, pp. 103–109.

14. Frank T. Cable, *The Birth and Development of the American Submarine*, p. 141.

15. Simon Lake, *Autobiography*, p. 79.

16. Simon Lake, *Argonaut*, pp. 1–32.

17. Lake Submarine Company document (1896).

18. Thomas A. E. Lake, interview with author, Stratford, Conn., Dec., 1972.

19. *Milford Citizen*, 1933 (galley proofs provided by T. A. E. Lake).

20. H. J. Miller to Simon Lake, May 28, 1909.

21. Barker, "Voyaging Under the Sea," pp. 195–209.

22. Marquis, *Who's Who in America, 1932–1933*, p. 310.

23. Simon Lake, *Autobiography*, pp. 125–27.

Chapter 4. Salvaging the Riches of the Sea

1. Lake Submarine Company, *Submarine Engineering*, pp. 1–7.

2. Ibid., p. 12.

3. Ibid., p. 10.

4. Simon Lake, *Submarine in War and Peace*, pp. 276–77.

5. Lonnquest, "Role of Simon Lake," pp. 84–85; Simon Lake, *Autobiography*, p. 138.

6. Simon Lake, *Autobiography*, p. 133; Lake Submarine Company, *Submarine Engineering*, pp. 8–11.

7. Simon Lake, *Autobiography*, pp. 135–36; Burgoyne, *Submarine Navigation*, vol. 1, pp. 252–53.

8. Simon Lake, *Autobiography*, p. 137.

9. *Connecticut Post*, Mar. 3, 1996.

10. Simon Lake to the Honorable John Q. Tilson, Apr. 26, 1930; *Bridgeport Sunday Post*, Mar. 6, 1955; George Smith, "Frederick the Great's Clock" (pamphlet).

11. Lake Submarine Company, *Submarine Engineering*, p. 31.

12. Ibid., pp. 33–34.

13. Morris, *John P. Holland*, p. 98.

14. Simon Lake to President William McKinley, 1899.

15. Simon Lake, *Under Water Torpedo Boats*, 1906, pp. 36–38.

16. Morris, *John P. Holland*, p. 91.

17. Prenliss, "American Submarine," p. 21.

18. Morris, *John P. Holland*, pp. 80–84.

19. Prenliss, "American Submarine," p. 18.

20. Morris, *John P. Holland*, pp. 102–103.

Chapter 5. The Plunger Affair

1. Robert Fine, *The Psychology of the Chess Player*, pp. 1–3.

2. E. T. Evans, *Dictionary of American Biography*, p. 541.

3. Morris, *John P. Holland*, pp. 96–97.

4. Ibid., pp. 111–12; John C. Lonnquest, "United States Submarine Procurement, 1900–1908: The Troubled Pathway to Fair Competition" (master's thesis, Duke University, 1989), p. 9.

5. E. B. Frost to Secretary of the Navy John D. Long, Mar. 3, 1900.

6. R. G. Skerrett, "The Relation of the Government to the Development of Submarine Vessels," *Scientific American* 21, supplement no. 1621 (Mar. 21, 1908): 180.

7. Ibid., p. 181.

8. Prenliss, "American Submarine," p. 19.

9. Skerrett, "Relation of the Government," p. 181.

10. Morris, *John P. Holland,* p. 104.

11. Compton-Hall, *Submarine Boats,* p. 33.

12. *Milford Citizen,* 1933.

13. Burgoyne, *Submarine Navigation,* vol. 1, pp. 263–69.

14. Simon Lake, *Autobiography,* pp. 198–202; Thomas A. E. Lake, interview with author, June, 1972.

15. U.S. House of Representatives, "United States Select Committee Under House Resolution 288," pp. 272–84.

16. Ibid., pp. 397–414.

17. Ibid., p. 4.

18. U.S. House of Representatives, "Testimony of Admiral Dewey," report of the Select Committee Appointed Pursuant to House Resolution 288, pp. 1–13.

19. Skerrett, "Relation of the Government," p. 182; Prenliss, "American Submarine," p. 22.

20. Skerrett, "Relation of the Government to the Development of Submarine Vessels," pp. 181–83.

21. U.S. House of Representatives, "Select Committee Under House Resolution 288," pp. 400–406.

22. R. G. Skerrett, "The History of the Competition" (manuscript in the files of the Submarine Force Library and Museum, Groton, Conn., 1905), p. 9.

23. Ibid., pp. 9–10.

24. Ibid., pp. 11–13.

25. Foster Voorhees to Simon Lake, Dec. 12, 1904.

26. Skerrett, "Relation of the Government," p. 12.

27. U.S. House of Representatives, "Select Committee Under House Resolution 288," pp. 414–15.

28. John C. Lonnquest, "United States Submarine Procurement," pp. 37–39.

29. John P. Holland to C. E. Foss, Chairman of the Committee on Naval Affairs, July 14, 1906.

Chapter 6. Off to Europe

1. J. C. Niven, C. Cangy, V. Welsh, and E. Nitsche, *Dynamic America,* p. 28.

2. Simon Lake, *Autobiography,* pp. 174–75.

3. *Milford Citizen,* 1933.

4. Ibid.

5. Norman Polmar and Jurrien Noot, *Submarines of the Russian and Soviet Navies, 1718–1990,* pp. 11–14.

6. Simon Lake to E. J. Hill, Aug. 11, 1906.

7. Polmar and Noot, *Submarines of the Russian and Soviet Navies,* pp. 14–15.

8. Ibid., p. 15.

9. Simon Lake, *Submarine in War and Peace,* pp. 63–73.

10. *Milford Citizen,* 1933.

11. Skerrett, "History of the Competition," p. 10.

12. Simon Lake to E. J. Hill, Aug. 11, 1906.

13. *Milford Citizen,* 1933.

14. Ibid.

15. Ibid.

16. Ibid.

17. U.S. Senate, "Hearings before the Committee on Naval Affairs of the Senate No. 395," (57th Cong., 1st sess.) p. 92.

18. *Milford Citizen*, 1933.

19. Ibid.

20. *National Cyclopaedia of American Biography*, pp. 5–7.

21. *Milford Citizen*, 1933.

22. Skerrett, "History of the Competition," pp. 9–10.

Chapter 7. Half a Submarine

1. Gaddis Smith, *Britain's Clandestine Submarines, 1914–1915*, pp. 86–151.

2. Arthur J. Marder, *From Dreadnought to Scapa Flow*, vol. 1, P. 330.

3. Simon Lake, *The Submarine in War and Peace*, pp. 25–26; Morris, *John P. Holland, Inventor of the Modern Submarine*, p. 52.

4. Arthur J. Marder, *From Dreadnought to Scapa Flow*, vol. 1, pp. 13, 332.

5. Ibid., pp. 13, 45, 332.

6. Gaddis Smith, *Britain's Clandestine Submarines, 1914–1915*, pp. 13–14.

7. Paul G. Halpern, *A Naval History of World War I*, p. 8; *Encyclopaedia Britannica*, 14th ed. (1936), p. 496.

8. Halpern, *Naval History*, p. 2.

9. Robert D. Evans, *An Admiral's Log*, p. 68.

10. Halpern, *Naval History*, p. 8; *Encyclopaedia Britannica*, 14th ed. (1936), p. 496; R. M. Grant, *U-Boats Destroyed: The Effects of Anti-Submarine Warfare, 1914–1918*, p. 16.

11. Gaddis Smith, *Britain's Clandestine Submarines*, p. 19.

12. Ibid., p. 21.

13. Ibid., pp. 31–33.

14. Ibid., p. 32.

15. Ibid., p. 38.

16. Ibid., pp. 88–90.

17. Arthur J. Marder, *From Dreadnought to Scapa Flow: The Royal Navy in the Fisher Era, 1904–1919*, vol. I, pp. 431–36.

18. Ibid., pp. 328–71.

19. Ibid., pp. 50–59; Simon Lake, "The Future of the Submarine," *The Optimist*, Nov., 1942, pp. 5–6.

20. Edward P. Stafford, *The Far and the Deep*, pp. 90–94; Marder, *From Dreadnought to Scapa Flow*, vol. 2, pp. 48–59.

21. Grant, *U-Boats Destroyed*, pp. 15–18.

22. Bernard Brodie, *A Layman's Guide to Naval Stretegy*, pp. 116–17.

23. Charles Seymour, *American Neutrality, 1914–1917*, pp. 74–86; Charles Mercer, "Who Could Sink the Lusitania?" *Boy's Life*, May, 1985, pp. 22–25, 60.

24. Simon Lake, *Autobiography*, pp. 250–51.

25. Ernest R. May, *The World War and American Isolation*, pp. 321–36.

26. James L. Mooney, *Dictionary of American Naval Fighting Ships*, vol. 2, p. 1.

27. *The Marine Review* 29, no. 15 (Apr. 14, 1904): 26.

28. Submarine Force Library and Museum, *Submarine Data;* Simon Lake, *Autobigraphy*, pp. 225–38.

29. *New York Herald*, May 7, 1916.

30. Norman Polmar and Thomas B. Allen, *Rickover: Controversy and Genius*, pp. 76–77.

31. Cable, *Birth and Development*, p. 288.

32. Morris, *John P. Holland*, p. 134.

33. Dwight R. Messimer, *The Merchant U-Boat: Adventures of the Deutschland, 1916–1918,* pp. 1–11.

34. Ibid., pp. 12–17, 59–62.

35. Ibid., pp. 11–36.

36. Simon Lake, *Autobiography,* p. 255.

37. Messimer, *Merchant U-Boat,* p. 59.

38. Simon Lake, *Autobiography,* pp. 255–56.

39. Ibid., p. 255.

40. Messimer, *Merchant U-Boat,* pp. 62–63.

41. Simon Lake, *Autobiography,* p. 257.

42. Messimer, *Merchant U-Boat,* pp. 60–61, 189–203.

43. Simon Lake, *Autobigraphy,* p. 258.

44. Stephen Roskill, *Naval Policy between the Wars,* Vol. 1, *The Period of Anglo-American Antagonism,* p. 19.

45. Ibid., pp. 20–23.

46. Ibid., p. 24.

47. Ibid., p. 31.

48. Simon Lake, *Autobiography,* p. 270.

49. Roskill, *Naval Policy,* p. 302.

50. Ibid., pp. 300–302.

51. Simon Lake, *Autobiography,* p. 268.

52. Quoted in ibid., pp. 312–29.

53. Ibid., p. 327.

54. Simon Lake to Lord Balfour, 1921.

55. Simon Lake, *Autobiography,* pp. 270–71.

56. Ibid., p. 266.

57. A. I. McKnee, "Development of Submarines in the United States," *Transactions of the American Society of Naval Engineers* 54 (1943): 344–55.

58. *Bridgeport Post,* Feb. 7, 1983.

59. *Bridgeport Times Star,* Feb. 5, 1932.

Chapter 8. Sunshine Homes and Concrete Pipes

1. Simon Lake, *Lakeolith Company Bulletin* (1920).

2. Simon Lake, *Autobiography,* p. 283.

3. Simon Lake, *Lakeolith: Hollow, Reinforced, Insulated Building Elements* (1920): 1–11.

4. Simon Lake, *Autobiography,* pp. 283–84.

5. Ibid., p. 284.

6. Ibid., pp. 283–84.

7. Simon Lake, *Lakeolith Company Bulletin* (1920).

8. Ibid.

9. Simon Lake to Col. K. M. Foss, Feb. 28, 1916.

10. *Bridgeport Post,* Mar. 3, 1939.

11. Ibid., Sept. 23, 1930.

12. Simon Lake to J. P. Holland, Jr., Feb. 15, 1916.

13. H. Van Deverrter (Kucher Airplane Company) to Simon Lake, July 16, 1929.

14. A. Gault to Simon Lake, Nov. 20, 1929.

15. *Bridgeport Post,* Nov. 16, 1969.

16. Simon Lake to Henry J. Miller, Nov. 28, 1929.

17. Simon Lake to Secretary of the Navy, Oct. 2, 1929.

18. Ibid.

19. Simon Lake, *Autobiography,* pp. 234–36.

20. Simon Lake to Secretary of the Navy, Oct. 2, 1929.

Chapter 9. North to the Pole

1. Simon Lake, *Autobiography,* pp. 288–90; Herman R. Friis, *United States Polar Expedition: National Archives Conference,* pp. 73–76; *Encyclopedia America,* International Edition (1993), "Hubert Wilkins," pp. 766–67.

2. Jules Vern, *The Omnibus Jules Vern,* p. 164.

3. Lowell Thomas, *Sir Hubert Wilkins: His World of Adventure,* pp. 8–41; Wilhjalmur Stefansson, *Northwest to Fortune,* pp. 250–55.

4. Thomas, *Sir Hubert Wilkins,* pp. 255–60.

5. Simon Lake, *Autobiography,* p. 288.

6. Ibid., pp. 289–90.

7. Simon Lake, "Modern Submarines in War and Peace-VII. Under-Ice Navigation with a Submarine," pp. 265–66.

8. Thomas, *Sir Hubert Wilkins,* pp. 261–62.

9. Ibid., pp. 265–66.

10. Thomas A. E. Lake to Editor of the *Bridgeport Post,* Apr. 27, 1930.

11. Ibid.

12. Ibid.

13. Ibid.

Chapter 10. The Search for HMS Hussar

1. Simon Lake, President's Statement to Stockholders, 1936.

2. Ibid.; Philip Carlson, interview with author, Worcester Museum, Worcester, Mass., June, 1996.

3. Simon Lake to A.D. Risteen, Director of Technical Research, The Traveler's Insurance Company, Apr. 21, 1930.

4. Ibid.

5. Ibid.

6. *Boston Transcript,* May 3, 1934.

7. *Bridgeport Post,* Dec. 8, 1934; Dorothy Needham, "The Dream That Had Fins," *Yankee Magazine,* Apr., 1974, pp. 76–82, 128–40; John J. Poluhowich, "The Quest for HMS *Hussar,*" *Connecticut Circle Magazine,* Spring, 1970, pp. 31–33.

8. *Bridgeport Post,* Sept. 26, 1936.

9. Ibid., Oct. 2, 1932; June 10, 1932; Nov. 6, 1931.

10. T. A. Heppenheimer, "To the Bottom of the Sea," *Invention and Technology,* Summer, 1992, pp. 28–38.

11. Ibid., Dec. 7, 1936; Mar. 18, 1937.

12. Ibid., Dec. 30, 1938.

13. Ibid., Jan. 18, 1940.

14. Ibid., June 24, 1937.

15. Ibid., Sept. 19, 1985.

Chapter 11. Dust

1. *Bridgeport Post,* Aug. 30, 1938.

2. Ibid., Apr. 15, 1940; *Bridgeport Times Star,* May 28, 1941.

3. *Bridgeport Post,* Dec. 20, 1940; Aug. 3, 1942.

4. *Bridgeport Times Star,* Jan. 18, 1941.

5. Simon Lake, *Autobiography,* pp. 1–303.

6. Ibid.

7. John Tierney, "The Invisible Force," *Science* 83 (Nov. 1983): 72–76; Simon Lake, confidential letter to the United States Navy, Mar. 14, 1942.

8. *Bridgeport Post,* July 29, 1939.

9. Ibid.

10. Ibid., July 9, 1921.

11. Simon Lake, *Autobiography,* p. 292.

12. Ibid., p. 292.

13. Ibid., p. 294.

14. Lonnquest, "Role of Simon Lake," p. 3.

Bibliography

Newspapers

Bridgeport Post.
Bridgeport Post Centennial.
Bridgeport Sunday Post.
Bridgeport Times Star.
Connecticut Post.
Milford Citizen. (Galley proofs of an article provided by T. A. E. Lake.)
New York Herald.

Works by Simon Lake

The Argonaut: Her Evolution and History, What She Was Built For and What She Has Accomplished. Atlantic Highlands, N.J.: Lake Submarine Company, 1899.
Company documents, 1896. In the files of the U.S. Submarine Force Library and Museum, Groton, Conn.
"The Future of the Submarine." *The Optimist,* November, 1942, pp. 5–6.
Lakeolith: Hollow, Reinforced, Insulated Building Elements. Stratford, Conn.: Lakeolith Company Catalog, 1920.
Letter to Lord Balfour. November 25, 1921. In the files of the U.S. Submarine Force Library and Museum, Groton, Conn.
Confidential letter to the U.S. Navy. March 14, 1942.
Letter from A. C. Gault to Simon Lake. November 20, 1929.
Letter to J. P. Holland, Jr. 1916. In the files of the U.S. Submarine Force Library and Museum, Groton, Conn.
Letter to Colonel K. M. Foss. February 28, 1916.
Letter to President William McKinley. Rough draft, undated except for year 1899. In the files of the U.S. Submarine Force Library and Museum, Groton, Conn.
Letter to Henry J. Miller. November 28, 1929.

Letter to A. D. Risteen, Director of Technical Research, The Travelers Insurance Company. April 21, 1930. In the files of the U.S. Submarine Force Library and Museum, Groton, Conn.

Letter to the Secretary of the Navy. 1929. In the files of the U.S. Submarine Force Library and Museum, Groton, Conn.

Letter to the Honorable John Q. Tilson. 1930. In the files of the U.S. Submarine Force Library and Museum, Groton, Conn.

"Modern Submarines in War and Peace." *International Marine Engineering* 20, 21 (July 1915–April 1916): 1–48.

President's Statement to Stockholders. Bridgeport, Conn.: Lake Submarine Salvage Corporation, 1936.

The Submarine in War and Peace. Philadelphia: J. B. Lippincott Company, 1918.

Submarine: The Autobiography of Simon Lake. New York: D. Appleton-Century Company, 1938.

Other Works

Barker, Ray Stannard. "Voyaging under the Sea. I. The Submarine Boat 'Argonaut' and Her Achievements." *McClure's Magazine,* January, 1899, pp. 195–209.

Beard, William E. "The Log of the C. S. Submarine." *Proceedings of the U.S. Naval Institute* 37 (1916): 1545–1557.

Brodie, Bernard. *A Layman's Guide to Naval Strategy.* Princeton, N.J.: Princeton University Press, 1942.

Burgoyne, Alan H. *Submarine Navigation, Past and Present.* Vols. 1 and 2. New York: E. P. Dutton and Company, 1903.

Cable, Frank T. *The Birth and Development of the American Submarine.* New York: Harper and Brothers, 1924.

Carlson, Philip. Interview with author. Worcester Museum, Worcester, Mass., June, 1996.

Cashman, Sean Dennis. *America in the Gilded Age.* New York: New York University Press, 1984.

Cervantes Saavedra, Miguel de. *Don Quixote de la Mancha.* New York: Halagon House, 1941.

Cocker, M. P. *Observer's Directory of the Royal Naval Submarines, 1901–1982.* London: Frederick Warne, 1982.

Compton–Hall, Richard. *Submarine Boats: The Beginnings of Underwater Warfare.* New York: Arco Publishing, 1983.

"Confederate Sub Sighted" (newsbrief). *Archaeology* 48, no. 5 (September–October, 1995): 17.

Cross, Wilbur. "Last Cruise of the Iron Witch." *True Magazine,* June, 1960, pp. 51–53, 105.

Encyclopaedia Britannica (14th Edition). London: Encyclopaedia Britannica Company, 1936.

Encyclopedia America (International Edition). Danbury, Conn.: Grolier, 1993.

Evans, E. T. *Dictionary of American Biography, 1941–1945.* New York: Charles Scribner's and Sons, 1973.

Evans, Robert D. *An Admiral's Log.* London: Appleton and Company, 1911.

Fine, Robert. *The Psychology of the Chess Player.* New York: Dover Publications, 1967.

Friis, Herman R. *United States Polar Expedition: National Archives Conference.* Athens: Ohio State University Press, 1970.

Frost, E. B. Letter to Secretary of the Navy John D. Long, March 3, 1900. In the files of the U.S. Submarine Force Library and Museum, Groton, Conn.

Grant, Robert. M. *U-Boats Destroyed: The Effects of Anti-Submarine Warfare, 1914–1918.* London: Putnam, 1964.

Grun, Bernard. *The Timetables of History.* New York: Simon and Schuster, 1979.

Gruse Harris, Patricia A. *Great Lake's First Submarine.* Michigan City, Mich.: Michigan City Historical Society, 1982.

Halpern, Paul G. *A Naval History of World War I.* Annapolis, Md.: Naval Institute Press, 1994.

Heppenheimer, T. A. "To the Bottom of the Sea." *Invention and Technology* 7 (Summer 1992): 28–38.

Holland, John P. "Submarine Navigation." *Cassier's Magazine* 12 (1897): 541–60.

———. Letter to C. E. Foss, Chairman of the Committee on Naval Affairs. In the files of the U.S. Submarine Force Library and Museum, Groton, Conn., 1906.

Horton, Edward. *The Illustrated History of the Submarine.* Garden City: Doubleday and Company, 1974.

Lake, Thomas A. E. Interviews with author. Stratford, Conn., 1970–74.

———. Letter to Editor of *Bridgeport Post,* April 27, 1930.

Lake Submarine Company. Papers of incorporation filed in the Borough of the Atlantic Highlands in the Township of Middletown, County of Monmouth, State of New Jersey, 1896. (Courtesy of T. A. E. Lake.)

———. *Submarine Engineering.* Bridgeport, Conn.: Lake Submarine Company, 1906.

Lake Torpedo Boat Company. *The Development of the Lake Type Submarine.* Bridgeport, Conn.: Lake Torpedo Boat Company, 1906.

———. *Under Water Torpedo Boats.* Bridgeport, Conn.: Lake Torpedo Boat Company, 1906.

Lonnquest, John C. "The Role of Simon Lake in the Development of the Modern Submarine." Undergraduate honors thesis, Washington College, 1981.

———. "United States Submarine Procurement, 1900–1908: The Troubled Pathway to Fair Competition." Master's thesis, Duke University, 1989.

Marder, Arthur J. *From Dreadnought to Scapa Flow: The Royal Navy in the Fisher Era, 1904–1919.* Vol. 1, *The Road to War.* London: Oxford University Press, 1961.

———. *From Dreadnought to Scapa Flow: The Royal Navy in the Fisher Era, 1904–1919.* Vol. 2, *The War Years: To the Eve of Jutland.* London: Oxford University Press, 1965.

Marine Review, The 29, no. 15 (April 14, 1904): 26.

Marquis, Albert Nelson. *Who's Who in America, 1932–1933.* Vol. 17. Chicago: A. N. Marquis Company, 1932.

May, Ernest R. *The World War and American Isolation.* Cambridge: Harvard University Press, 1959.

McKnee, A. I. "Development of Submarines in the United States." *Transactions of the American Society of Naval Engineers* 54 (1943): 344–55.

Mercer, Charles. "Who Could Sink the Lusitania?" *Boy's Life,* May, 1985, pp. 22–25, 60.

Messimer, Dwight R. *The Merchant U-Boat: Adventures of the Deutschland, 1916–1918.* Annapolis, Md.: Naval Institute Press, 1988.

Miller, H. J. Letter to Simon Lake. May, 28, 1909. In the files of the U.S. Submarine Force Library and Museum, Groton, Conn.

Mooney, James L. *Dictionary of American Naval Fighting Ships.* Vol. 2. Washington, D.C.: Naval Department Office of the Chief of Naval Operations, Naval History Division, 1963.

Morris, Richard K. *John P. Holland, 1841–1914: Inventor of the Modern Submarine.* Annapolis, Md.: United States Naval Institute, 1966.

National Cyclopaedia of American Biography. New York: James T. Wilhite and Company, 1916.

National Press Reporter 16, no. 12 (May, 1914).

Needham, Dorothy. "The Dream That Had Fins." *Yankee Magazine,* April, 1974, pp. 76–82, 128–40.

Niven, J. C., V. Welsh, and E. Nitsche. *Dynamic America*. New York: General Dynamics Corporation and Doubleday and Company, 1960.

Parsons, William Barclay. *Robert Fulton and the Submarine*. New York: Columbia University Press, 1922.

Polmar, Norman, and Thomas B. Allen. *Rickover: Controversy and Genius*. New York: Simon and Schuster, 1982.

Polmar, Norman, and Jurrien Noot. *Submarines of the Russian and Soviet Navies, 1718–1990*. Annapolis, Md.: Naval Institute Press, 1991.

Poluhowich, John J. "Bridgeport's Submarine Pioneer." *LISA/86 Festival Magazine* (*Long Island Sound Festival Magazine*), 1986, pp. 46–48.

———. "The Quest for HMS *Hussar.*" *Connecticut Circle Magazine* 33 (Spring, 1970): 31–33.

Prenliss, Knut. "The American Submarine." Manuscript in the National Archives (RG 45), Naval Records Collection of the Office of Naval Records and Library, Washington, D.C., 1947.

Roland, Alex. *Underwater Warfare in the Age of Sail*. Bloomington: Indiana University Press, 1978.

Roskill, Stephen. *Naval Policy between the Wars*. Vol. 1, *The Period of Anglo-American Antagonism*. New York: Walker and Company, 1968.

Seymour, Charles. *American Neutrality, 1914–1917*. Hamden, Conn.: Archon Books, 1967.

Skerrett, R. G. "The History of the Competition." Manuscript in the files of the Submarine Force Library and Museum, Groton, Conn., 1905 (?).

———. "The Relation of the Government to the Development of Submarine Vessels." *Scientific American* 21, Supplement No. 1621 (March 21, 1908): 180–81.

Smith, Gaddis. *Britain's Clandestine Submarines, 1914–1915*. New Haven: Yale University Press, 1964.

Smith, George. "Alexander the Great's Clock" (pamphlet). Milford, Conn.: George Smith and Sons Funeral Home, ca. 1965.

Stafford, Edward P. *The Far and The Deep*. New York: G. P. Putnam's Sons, 1967.

Stefansson, Wilhjalmur. *Northwest to Fortune*. Westport, Conn.: Greenwood Press, 1958.

Submarine Exploration and Recovery Company. *Recovering the Natural Resources of the Sea*. Bridgeport, Conn.: Submarine Exploration and Recovery Company, 1920.

Submarine Force Library and Museum. *Submarine Data*. New London, Conn.: Submarine Library and Museum, 1965.

Sueter, Murray F. *The Evolution of the Submarine Boat, Mine and Torpedo.* Portsmouth, England: J. Griffin and Co., 1908.

Sweeney, James B. *A Pictorial History of Oceanographic Submersibles.* New York: Crown Publishers, 1970.

Thomas, Lowell. *Sir Hubert Wilkins: His World of Adventure.* New York: McGraw-Hill, 1961.

Tierney, John. "The Invisible Force." *Science* 83 (November, 1983): 72–76.

U.S. House of Representatives. House Select Committee under House Resolution 288 (60th Cong., 1st sess). Hearings Beginning 9 March 1908. Washington, D.C.: Government Printing Office, 1908.

U.S. Senate. Hearings before the Committee on Naval Affairs of the Senate No. 395. (57th Cong., 1st sess). Washington, D.C.: Government Printing Office, 1902.

Van Deverrter, H. Kucher Airplane Company letter to Simon Lake. July 16, 1929. In the files of the U.S. Submarine Force Library and Museum, Groton, Conn.

Verne, Jules. *The Omnibus Jules Verne.* Philadelphia: J. B. Lippincott Co., 1900.

Voorhees, Foster. Letter to Simon Lake. February 3, 1904. In the files of the U.S. Submarine Force Library and Museum, Groton, Conn.

Walker, Gladys. "From Turtle to Trident." *Connecticut Magazine,* Summer, 1970, pp. 34–40.

Index

Note: Pages with illustrations are indicated by italics.